A Wise Woman Builds Her House

One Woman's Journey
Every Woman's Divine Destiny

Charisse M. Gibert

xulon
PRESS

Dedication

To my 3 little wise women in training Chloe, Chai and Chari; To my son Joshua, who knows a wise woman when he sees one – Thank You for giving mommy private time to write- I love you all! To my husband, Elder Benjamin A. Gibert, my partner in purpose, whom I love, respect, and admire. Thank you for your love, support and understanding during this 12 year labor of love.

Acknowledgements

To Rev. Robert Prelow, a true prophet of God, who released a destiny seed into my life, while I was yet a teen – that one day I would write books that would bless the Body of Christ;

To my parents, Dalbert and Cheryl Galloway; and to my sister and brother, Shauna & Orlando Williams – Thank you for your love and encouragement;

To all of the wise women who have profoundly impacted my life: my mommy – Cheryl L. Galloway, my grandmothers: Nadine Avery & Clara Westbrook, my great-grandmother: Marguerite Williams; to my two spiritual mothers, Dr. Bridget Hilliard (New Light Christian Center Church, Houston, TX.) and Pastor Gael Wallace (Detroit World Outreach, Detroit, MI).

Table of Contents

FOREWORD

Your Offering, Your Skill, Your Obedience - God's House

Exodus 35:5

> *Take ye from among you an offering unto the LORD:*
> *whosoever is of a willing heart, let him bring it, an*
> *offering of the LORD; gold, and silver, and brass . . .*

When God desired to build his holy tabernacle, He knew exactly what he wanted it to look like. Neither man nor woman was qualified to determine its design, construction or layout. Yet God allowed man to become involved by providing him with some key components that were necessary in the construction of the temple: his offering, his skill, and his obedience. By providing them with these tools, man now had a God approved way to join in and help with the building construction.

One of the first things that God commanded Moses to do in the temple construction was to receive an offering from the Israelites. Some of the offerings that they brought were tangible things of value: gold, silver, brass, fine linens, animal skins, rare woods, anointing oils & spices, incense, gems, and stones. Anyone who had these divinely requested items in their possession could give them as an offering, as long as they gave from a willing heart.

A willing heart has no hidden or personal agendas. It is a heart that submits and obeys the word, will, and way of God. A heart that says not my will, but your will be done Lord. Ultimately, it is a heart that says God knows what is best, so I will do it His way.

Exodus 35:29

> *The children of Israel brought a willing offering unto the LORD, every man and woman, whose heart made them willing to bring for all manner of work, which the LORD had commanded to be made by the hand of Moses.*

The second part of the command called upon the men and women of Israel who had skill to make what God had commanded. Both the men and women possessed skills that were both valuable and necessary for the Lord to use in His temple building. The Bible also says that the women who were "wise hearted" or whose heart "stirred them up in wisdom" spun with their hands.

Essentially, both the material offerings and the offerings of craftsmanship were to be given from a heart that was willing to obey God's specific instructions. God not only had a plan for the children of Israel collectively, he also had a specific plan for each individual. One such individual was Bezalel.

God's plan for him was to be a master craftsman, designer, and embroiderer, with skills so excellent that he could teach others to do the same. As a result of Bezalel's willing heart, the Lord increased him by pouring out His wisdom, knowledge, and understanding upon him, so that this man was able to create and design things that no one had probably ever seen.

God's plan is that we all act as Bezalel did. He wants us to be willing to do His will, so that He can increase us in the things that He has called us to do by pouring out his knowledge, wisdom and understanding upon us. Then, He wants us to use His knowledge, wisdom, and understanding to build our homes according to His specifications.

Proverbs 14:1

> *Every wise woman buildeth her house: but the fool-*
> *ish plucketh it down with her hands.*

Ultimately, God knows what He wants our households to look like and how He desires for them to function. And when we allow His word, will, and way to penetrate our hearts and influence our actions, we are able to build an excellent home that can't be destroyed by issues, situations, lies, or any other ungodly influence.

Over 12 years ago, I gave my willing heart as an offering to the Lord. I desired for the Lord to teach me how to build an excellent home where God would want to dwell. I desperately desired to do it His way. I tried my way, and it wasn't working. I asked for the Lord to pour out his knowledge, wisdom, and understanding to me concerning this issue. It was during this time that He gave me the wisdom principles outlined in this book.

As I sow this book into the kingdom of God, I pray that the Lord would birth in you a desire, hunger, intense dedication and commitment to apply the wisdom of God as you construct a household that brings Him glory.

I have sought His wisdom, I have worked His wisdom and now His wisdom is a part of me.

INTRODUCTION

Searching For My Dream Home

I love beautiful homes. As a young girl, I used to visit model homes with my mom and sister. These luxury model homes were often 2 to 3 times larger than our home, professionally decorated, and full of some of the finest custom amenities that we dreamed of having.

When I visited these models, I wasn't going with the intention to buy one. I had neither the resources, nor the use for one - I was still in high school. Instead, my intention was to visit them and imagine myself living in one in the future. Each time I visited a model, I thought about how I would decorate, accessorize, and position the furniture.

Though the models became more extravagant through the years, I always felt that there was always something missing. If only the model had another bedroom, a larger kitchen, or more windows, I contemplated.

So with each year of looking and taking mental notes, I began to develop a picture of what I wanted my house to look like. Interestingly, it didn't look like any of the other homes in totality. It was actually a culmination of what I considered to be the best of each home, in addition to the special things I desired.

Before long, I had captured the very essence of the perfect home in my mind. From that point on, there wasn't a new design or idea that could influence me to change the overall picture of my potential dream home. I knew *exactly* what I wanted.

Similarly, when I got married, I knew exactly what I wanted. I wanted to be like the awesome woman of God illustrated in Proverbs 31. I looked at all of her wonderful achievements and how well she was received, respected and rewarded. I desired that. I longed to be received by the Lord as a wise and virtuous woman. I wanted the respect of my husband, love from my children and others alike.

I wanted gifts and encouraging words to be lavished upon me because of my efforts and accomplishments. I wanted the reward of the woman who excelled in all of her God-given responsibilities and endeavors. I wanted the reward of a woman who took care of her household, blessed her family, had a superior business mind, and ministered with wisdom. I also wanted to avoid massive arguments, do as I pleased (as much as possible), and have my "own" things that my husband couldn't touch. In essence, I wanted to be in control.

However, within the first few months of marriage, I felt as if I had ended up with a stubborn man of God who communicated when he felt like it, opposed many of my ideas, and who wanted me to be a carbon copy of him. In combative form, I developed a plan, independent of God's wisdom, of how I wanted my household to run. I figured that *if he wasn't going to get the job done like I wanted it done, I'd do it myself.* Before I knew it, I began to see myself as the head of our household and then actually tried to establish myself as such.

I wasn't loud or boisterous. I never embarrassed him in public. I just harbored what I call a "quiet rebellion" and executed "gentle manipulation". No matter what it's called — it was wrong and I was headed down the road of marital destruction.

There was no way in the kingdom of God that I was going to get any reward acting out like I did. In my heart, I wanted better. I expected better, but I also knew that I wasn't going to let "a man" (even though he was my husband) control me. I was going to be an "independent married woman", so to speak.

Society, the wisdom of the world, told me to control my own

life. Although I believed the world didn't have the answer, I knew its wisdom too well. Through the years, I heard enough wives express feelings of not being appreciated and I determined in my heart what I would and wouldn't tolerate.

Yet, I wanted to know what I was supposed to do, capable of doing, anointed to do, or something. I desperately needed a revelation of my role as wife from the Lord, not from my husband. So, I fasted, prayed, and God answered.

As the Lord dealt with me, I knew that I had to be honest with Him and myself. First, I had to evaluate my attitude, thoughts, and intentions in my marriage. Second, I had to accept the fact that my plans weren't working because they not rooted in His wisdom. I could no longer haphazardly apply the Word of God in my marriage and receive the blessing of the Lord. Neither could I rely upon my plan or the mediocre marriage examples of others to become a model for me to spec in establishing my own marriage.

The more I read what the Word had to say about marriage and being a wife, I realized that my dream of what a household ought to be was a collage of some good examples, my desires and the world's wisdom. What I thought I wanted wasn't completely in line with God's plan for my marriage life.

As I searched the Word, I came upon Proverbs 14:1:

> **Every wise woman buildeth her house: but the foolish plucketh it down with her hands.**

After meditating and studying this scripture, the Lord gave me a revelation and began unfolding his plan concerning the how-to's of building my house. Then, he showed me that if I would walk in it with diligence that this revelation and my testimony could help wives throughout the Body of Christ become women who abandoned the wisdom of the world, established their homes in the wisdom of God, and obtained an abundantly blessed marriage and family life.

With relentless faith, I did what the Lord told me to do. I took God's plan for my marriage and household and engrafted them into my life. I allowed God to show me who I was and what I needed to do in order to become who He wanted me to be.

Use this book as a tool to help establish your marriage and family life according to the Word of God. As you apply the biblical principles associated with it, the wisdom of God will minister divine direction to you for your own household. You are anointed to build!

Note: The women in this book are fictitious; however their thoughts and actions represent the carnal mindset and fleshly attitudes that many women of God have functioned with or do function with on a daily basis.

PART 1

PRE-FAB HOMES

ERECTING WALLS

As a young Christian, a number of dysfunctional relationships affected my expectations of marriage early in life. Some of the dysfunction I viewed on television, some of it I gathered from friends or strangers, and the rest was media based stories or worldly representations of marriage. I was affected by the:

- tears of mistreated, neglected, controlled, abused and under appreciated, wives

- vindictive women who punished their abusive husbands by destroying their property, publicly exposing their character in the workplace or attempting murder

- women who said never trust a man, including your husband

- women who said all men cheat, you may as well accept that

- men of God yelling, cursing, and disrespecting their wives in public.

- drug riddled ministers children instilling fear in their godly parents as they demanded drug money and stole from them

- lack of positive communication and continuous fighting and arguing

- strangers who said awful things about their husbands and joked about their inadequacies

- unsolicited marriage counsel and advice from those who experienced many trials and errors and believed that they had "wisdom" (apart from God's word)

As a result, I came away from all of this exposure with several conclusions:

1. Very few people had a marriage worth modeling.

2. Church people were not immune to dysfunctional households.

3. Due to the large quantity of counterfeit marriage examples, I didn't see much difference between a saved person's marriage and a non-believer's marriage.

4. There had to be something better, I just hadn't seen it yet.

Choosing to believe the latter of my conclusions, I began really observing my parents marriage and the marriage of my pastor and his wife. In doing so, I learned that when 2 people submit to one another and allow the Lord to be their head – divorce isn't even an option. I realized early on that Holy Spirit intervention and obedience to the Lord and His word saves marriages.

As a young girl, I was faced with a challenge. I began to consider what to believe and act upon for my life and future marriage: the wealth of negative worldly marital examples or the pocketful of spirit-led ones. I really wanted to see more successful and abundantly blessed marriages.

Yet, I took the convenient route. I allowed other's negative experiences counsel me and dictate much of what I would believe about marriage. Eventually, I rationalized that if I could protect myself from the ills of marriage by doing whatever was necessary, then I could successfully establish my own.

ULTIMATUMS
Threats which if not given into, will be followed by war

The years of storing notes about poor marriage and family relationships began to produce an attitude that only God could deliver me from. You see, I determined in my mind what I would and wouldn't accept, what I'd do and wouldn't do, what I'd tolerate and wouldn't tolerate. I made all of these decisions before I had a spouse or even a potential one.

Each decision that I made became a brick that I used to form a wall around my heart. I convinced myself by putting up a defense system around my heart, that no one and nothing would hurt me. My husband couldn't get in unless I let him get in. He couldn't effect my emotions unless I let him. He couldn't even make me laugh unless I wanted to laugh. I was in control, so I thought.

For me, the wall symbolized the strength of my will. I put so much thought and effort into building these walls before I got married that I wasn't going to tear them down for anyone, not even my husband.

Armed with more worldly counsel on marriage than the counsel of the Lord, I approached some aspects of our marriage from behind these walls. When I perceived that my feelings could get hurt, I was about to face some marital disappointments, or I felt underappreciated, I would launch an ultimatum.

These ultimatums were like missiles that I launched when I needed to keep my husband at a far enough distance from my heart. One incident that called for such an attack occurred when my husband took for granted something that I did around the house.

Taken For Granted No More

One day after straightening up our bedroom, I noticed that my husband went back and forth from the bathroom to his dresser to get hair products, cologne, toothbrushes and toothpaste. All the room to room action seemed to waste some of his time. Plus, I believed that those things belonged in the bathroom, since they could spill and possibly ruin the dresser or the carpet.

So I put all of his toiletries in their proper place - the bathroom. The new arrangement saved him some time, but he didn't acknowledge what I had done. After using the items, he would place them back on his dresser - where he didn't find them.

I went on for a couple more months re-positioning the items. Every morning after he left for work, I would take the items off of his dresser - giving him more room for things that belonged there - and I would place his toiletries in the bathroom. Yet he still hadn't acknowledged it.

Finally one day, I had enough. I saw the items back on his dresser – but this time, I left them there. My mind began pulling up all of the data that I had placed in my heart about husbands taking their wives for granted. The wall around my heart was wavering and I didn't want to get hurt, so I launched an ultimatum, a threat.

This may sound strange to some, but many of you know exactly what I'm talking about. When my husband came home from work, I waited for him to go into the bedroom to change clothes. When he did, I repositioned the items where they belonged. I cleaned hard. I slammed bottles, cans, and boxes. I figured that since he hadn't noticed what was going on, he needed to actually see what I did each morning.

When he asked what was wrong, I told him that I felt he took my efforts for granted. Then I told him to take a good look at what I had done and where I put everything, because I would never do it again!

As I ended the conversation, I let him know that if he wouldn't appreciate the things that I did around the house, then he could wash his own clothes - and he did for weeks. But then the Lord began to speak to me. He showed me three things about attitude and my intentions:

1. The ultimatums that I designed to protect myself had the potential to destroy me and my household.

2. The threats weren't to my husband, but toward GOD. It was as if I was saying, "Lord, I'm not going to do this, this, and this."

3. God assigned the task of helpmeet to me as a wife, whether I felt I was compensated by my husband or not.

I had to do something different. I was on a broad road to marital chaos.

PRE-FABBIN' IT

Most pre-fabricated homes are fully or partially constructed in a factory. Research shows that in the year 2000, one out of six first time home buyers built pre-manufactured homes for three main reasons: cost, control and convenience.

Cost
    Pre-fabricated homes are affordable. They often cost less than the traditionally built home because they don't have a deep foundation, but rather a shallow or less durable one.

Control
    Unlike traditional home buyers, a manufactured home buyer can determine what kind of materials (wood, cinder block or concrete) they want to use to build their foundation. Some say that this gives the buyer more control over what part of the building process to spend their money.

Convenience
    The option to buy a new home that costs less and is almost hassle free is an attractive one. The simplicity of going into a showroom, choosing a model, working out the payments, and getting a build date is as easy as it gets.

My Cost, My Control, My Convenience

Whether I realized it or not, as a new home builder, I began building my home the pre-fab way. I had a lot of cost tied up in my building project. In fact, my home was partially constructed before I even had a mate. I'd stashed years of worldly views on marriage and family life to the point that I had walls and weapons (ultimatums) already on hand.

I believed that I controlled the quality of my married life. With the walls pre-built, I had a sense of control - quality control. When I felt the need, I'd conveniently throw a wall up. I knew what the outcome would be in whatever situation we encountered, because I set the standards with each wall I erected. Neither my husband nor my environment could strongly influence **my will**. Whether I chose to act upon my will or not wasn't the point, it was the fact that I had empowered myself to do as I pleased.

However, the problem with this whole train of thought was that the Word of God didn't bear witness with it. Two scriptures circulated throughout my mind as I was going through this situation:

Proverbs 19:21

> *There are many devices in a man's heart; nevertheless the counsel of the LORD, that shall stand.*

Proverbs 16:25

> *There is a way that seemeth right unto a man, but the ends thereof are the ways of death.*

My way seemed to be the right way, but my methods weren't helping to improve my marriage. I had many devices, but not enough counsel from the Lord. The only difference between my house building efforts and the way an unbeliever constructed her home was the fact that I accepted Jesus as my Savior and the unbeliever hadn't. Both of us were using the same materials to build our homes - the wisdom of the world.

I loved the Lord and I believed the Word of God, but I didn't know what it had to say about building a home. I was familiar with the scripture that talked about the wise and the foolish builder, but I wanted to find something more specific. At the time, I needed something that had the word "woman" in it.

As I searched the Word, the Lord began to speak to me through Proverbs 14:1 and the parable of the wise and foolish builder. Upon meditating these scriptures, I realized that even though I threw up walls at every whim, I wasn't building a thing. My actions were actually counter productive.

When a builder constructs a home, they lay a foundation before they build the house. The foundation must be constructed of materials that can support the framework of the house. He can't just lay a foundation with anything he feels like and then haphazardly build upon it.

But, that's precisely what I did. The ultimatums and the pre-constructed walls were established upon the world's wisdom. The Word of God couldn't support worldly wisdom. My house was destined for a fall unless I began using the Word to build upon the Word.

1 Corinthians 3:10

> *According to the grace of God which is given unto me, as a wise master builder, I have laid the foundation, and another buildeth thereon. But let every man take heed how he buildeth thereupon.*

WHO'S BUILDING WHAT?

The Builder & The Building

Let me start by saying that the devil is a liar. The Bible calls him the father of lies. He is the ultimate deceiver. One of the biggest lies the enemy has channeled through women in the world has become a weapon he uses in his arsenal against home and family. He has persuaded women and their movements to pull these lies from his arsenal and aim them at God's establishment of marriage and family.

One such lie that must be destroyed says that women don't have a place of power in society, neither in their marriages, therefore they must take it. This is a lie for many different reasons.

1. God created a system of order to protect everyone within the chain of authority
2. No one is considered lowly on the chain, because God created mankind to submit one to another
3. God called wives and husbands to take dominion together, not independent of one another
4. The husband and wife have powerful roles, each being necessary and significant in successfully accomplishing the plan of God in victory

The truth of the matter is that both men and women are supposed to build the home together. Both of them possess significant, yet different roles which are necessary in establishing household excellence.

Yet, there are cases where the husband is not walking in his role and the woman is left trying to assume his position. And there are cases where the wife isn't walking in her role and the husband is left helpless. In essence, there are homes in which one or the other is building, while the other is hindering or destroying the building process.

This isn't the pattern that God left for us to follow. God created the two roles to harmoniously function together under his specific direction and instruction to draw unbelieving men and women to him. Our marriages and families are to command the attention of the unbeliever and draw them to the Lord. God's plan is that we look at how he built his family and then pattern our building efforts after it.

In Jesus Name, You Can Do It!

Potential is Dormant Power that must be activated in order to Produce Excellence

God has placed within every woman the potential to build and establish a home according to His word. However, this power lies dormant until she allows God to activate it in at least 4 ways.

- Believe/Confess Jesus as Savior - Rom. 10:9-10
- Receive Power of God - Acts 1:8

- Walk in the principles of God - James 1:22
- Go forth in your God-given role – Genesis 2:18

Some Christian women have accomplished at least 3 of the things above. Yet, the enemy has successfully persuaded countless others to stop progressing after having attained one or two of the four things. They have bought the lie that if they help their husbands and support their endeavors, they will lose ground, but their spouses will advance.

As a result, many of us haven't gone forth in one of our God ordained roles as help meet. So, we don't have the capability to produce excellent marriages and families. Our building potential is hampered when we don't function in this purpose.

What's a help meet? One day God simplified this term for me. To help means to assist. So to be a help meet means that wives are to meet their husbands wherever they are and then assist them as the two take dominion together.

In other words, God designed wives to meet husbands at their point of; strength, weakness, insecurity, shame, doubt, guilt, failure, success, or whatever state they are in to further help them, so that together they can succeed and claim victory in life.

Most women can easily identify with their desire to be in power, but many, out of ignorance, don't know what to do to obtain and walk in it. Instead, they want to take a short cut. Many wives take the short cut because they don't want to help their husbands do anything. They don't think he needs their help. They believe he has enough help of his own. So, they want to take dominion without him. They don't want to meet him where he is to help him, but to ridicule him.

Building Elements: Wisdom, Understanding & Knowledge

Proverbs 24:3,4

Through wisdom is an house builded; and by under-standing it is established: And by knowledge shall the chambers be filled with all precious and pleasant riches.

The Builder: Wisdom

There are 3 essential components to building a household of excellence: wisdom, understanding and knowledge. Though the world places knowledge above all, the Bible lists wisdom as the principal building element.

When God established the heavens and founded the earth, he used wisdom. When we get ready to build our homes, we must employ wisdom. Wisdom builds excellent houses. Wisdom transforms ordinary homes into extraordinary household, homes, marriages and families.

Within the framework of this book, the term "house" will include the combined covenant relationships: husband, wife, children as well as the spiritual relationships with God (Father, Son, and Holy Spirit).

In the context of wisdom used for building or constructing a home, the Hebrew word is chokmah. Chokmah means skill in war, wisdom in administration, acting wisely.

Therefore, in order for a woman to build her home in excellence, she must:

- Adapt the skills necessary to obtain and nurture relationships within the home
- Apply the Word (the wisdom of God) to her daily life
- Do what the Word says to do: Obey it

God has given us several scriptures that illustrate the relationship between women, building, and the wisdom of God. Here are a few:

Proverbs 9:1a
Wisdom hath builded her house, she hath hewn out her seven pillars:
Truth: Wisdom builds

Proverbs 14:1
Every wise woman buildeth her house: but the foolish plucketh it down with her hands.
Truth: Woman uses wisdom to build

Proverbs 31:26a
> *She openeth her mouth with wisdom . . .*
>
> **Truth: Woman's heart is full of the Word; Her mouth expresses it**

The Concrete: Understanding

When a builder wants to build her house, she starts by digging a hole to lay the foundation. Most people will tell you that this is one of the most costly parts of the house building process, because it is the most laborious. But once that hole has been dug to the proper specifications, the foundation can be laid properly.

Concrete is the basic material used in a foundation. Before concrete is mixed with water, it is simply a dry compound composed of pulverized rock and other rock-like sediments. Yet, when water is added and the solution is thoroughly stirred, and properly poured, the mixture solidifies. Once the concrete has set, the builder can begin to put up the framework of her house.

Godly understanding is like concrete. When the principles of God are mixed with obedience, the result is understanding. God gives us (Believers) his wisdom freely throughout the Word. He even tells us that if we lack it, to just ask. However, understanding is not given to us without an effort; it must be produced by our obedience to the Word.

A woman of God who desires to build her home according to her own wishes and desires is planning to fail. In essence, she doesn't have the essential ingredients for a solid concrete foundation. She hasn't dug deep. In other words, she hasn't:

- Deemed it necessary to ask, seek or knock in order to obtain godly principles that pertain to establishing an excellent home

- Obeyed the Word concerning the principles of God she is already familiar with concerning marriage and family

There are only 2 types of foundations to build upon. There is the one made of rock and the one made of earth. The rock symbolizes

Jesus Christ and his teachings and the earth symbolizes worldly teachings (doctrine).

When I began throwing up the walls on my spiritually pre-fabbed home, I didn't build with the intention to dig deep. I was just trying to get my house up. I thought that since I was a Believer, and I loved the Lord, that I had a foundation that was already laid: Jesus.

But, my foundation was a mess. Have you ever seen concrete that wasn't mixed properly? Sometimes the mixture lacked adequate water, sometimes it wasn't stirred thoroughly. Either way, it was a lumpy, crusty mess that could fall apart if under enough pressure. There were holes all in the mixture.

That's precisely what type of foundation that I had. I obeyed some of what the Lord told me to do, but other times I rationalized and did what I wanted to do in the midst of tough situations. I had some principles, mixed with worldly wisdom and inconsistent obedience to the godly principles, which didn't produce adequate understanding to have a rock solid foundation.

Luke 6:47-49

> *Whosoever cometh to me, and heareth my sayings, and doeth them, I will shew you to whom he is like: He is like a man which built an house, and digged deep, and laid the foundation on a rock: and when the flood arose, the stream beat vehemently upon that house, and could not shake it: for it was founded upon a rock.*

> *But he that heareth, and doeth not, is like a man that without a foundation built an house upon the earth; against which the stream did beat vehemently, and immediately it fell; and the ruin of that house was great.*

The Finisher: Knowledge

Knowledge is the Finisher of your Household

Knowledge consists of information that has been mentally processed, stored, and in many cases experienced. The world says that knowledge is power. But the truth of the matter is that knowledge (a treasury of processed information) void of godly insight (wisdom) has no power. Yet when God gives his insight into what you have learned, revelation takes place and your life is transformed.

Once a woman of God begins to obey godly principles and gains understanding of those principles, on-going knowledge is necessary to enhance the internal value of the home. The academic arena calls it continuing education. This further consistent gathering of knowledge must be a regular course of action.

Proverbs 24:4
> *And by knowledge shall the chambers be filled with all precious and pleasant riches.*

Proverbs 19:2a
> *Also, that the soul be without knowledge, it is not good . . .*

Godly Insight on My Cooking Knowledge

I have over 25 years of experience cooking good food. Over the years, I've read thousands of articles on eating healthy. I've even watched thousands of cooking shows to learn more about different foods, their nutritional properties, vitamins and minerals, and healthy alternatives to otherwise unhealthily prepared foods.

Often, I would learn much of this information, but my mind processed only a portion of it. This information became a source of inspiration to cook creatively as I used various herbs and seasonings to accent the flavor of our food.

I didn't automatically possess power when I gathered this information, because knowledge isn't power. But when I began to ask the Lord to give me wisdom and to help me to become an excellent home chef, He gave me wisdom.

He told me to begin preparing our food using one of the healthiest varieties of oil, olive oil. Then he told me to forsake canned foods and use predominately fresh or frozen. He told me that he would teach me how to cook frozen foods and make them taste like they came out of a garden – and He did. I then began to change my vegetable preparation methods and began stir-frying or sautéing predominately. As a result, our food looked livelier, veggies looked brighter, and everything tasted even better and retained more nutritional value.

Without any information or knowledge on cooking or food preparation, there would have been no basis for God to breathe his wisdom upon. Just as I sought the Lord on being a more excellent home chef, God expects us to seek his wisdom on everything that pertains to managing and establishing a household. He wants to manifest himself in our everyday affairs.

It's not God's will for us to struggle in life from day to day. Neither is it the will of God for us to just exist in our households and not partake in building them according to his specifications.

Sources of Information

Now there are 2 sources of information that we can choose to store in our minds: word-based/biblical information designed to produce success and prosperity in our lives and information gleaned from trial and error (void of godly wisdom).

The biblical information that we have in storage will only become powerful in our lives once we take it out and begin to use it or walk in it. If we just continue to store information, but never use it - we will never fully experience the abundant lifestyle that God promised.

The Bible tells us that there are some who are ever learning, but never coming to the knowledge of the truth. That word knowledge is a word that means to intimately know - having experienced it, used it or applied it.

That is why some Christian women can be saved for 10, 15, 20 years and struggle in their marriages and family relationships. They sat in church and gathered the Word for years, but never fully utilized it and asked or believed the Lord to give revelation and direction from it.

They merely took a step here or there with it, but they never walked in it. God is a God of love and his plan is to prosper us, but if we just keep gathering information without the intent to use it – we won't achieve the level of good success described in His word.

Choices Choices Choices:
Converting Information into Knowledge

There are only two types of information that a Believer will learn and store as knowledge in the treasure of her heart: information (biblical principles, commandments, teachings) in line with the Word and information contrary to the Word.

Jeremiah 21:8

> *And unto this people thou shalt say, Thus saith the LORD; Behold, I set before you the way of life, and the way of death.*

Information in line with the Word that has been learned and acted upon is good and leads to life. On the path of life there is health, vitality and prosperity. However carnal information void of God's wisdom leads to death. On the path of death are destruction, ruin and chaos. The Bible teaches us that if we don't gain the biblical knowledge necessary to walk on the path that leads to life, then we put ourselves in a position to be destroyed.

Jesus came so that we would have life and have it more abundantly. God wants us to choose life, but it is our choice. Each day we must choose to either walk in godly wisdom or foolishness.

The Bible tells us that wisdom calls out to us in order to direct us to the path of life. He speaks direction. He speaks encouragement. He sends godly people around you that walk in his counsel to counsel you. He does all of this because he wants you to make the right choice – choice that leads to an abundant life:

Proverbs 8:1-5

> *Doth not wisdom cry? and understanding put forth*

her voice? She standeth in the top of high places, by the way in the places of the paths. She crieth at the gates, at the entry of the city, at the coming in at the doors. Unto you, O men, I call; and my voice is to the sons of man. O ye simple, understand wisdom: and, ye fools, be ye of an understanding heart.

Once wisdom has called out to us, we can choose it and obtain God's promises or heed the voice of foolishness, and neglect the promises of God. Some of us would assume that the Believer would choose life - but many of us don't. When wisdom calls, we rationalize. We don't even know his voice, because we don't know his Word. So, we give every reason under the sun why we shouldn't do what the Lord God has spoken to us to do.

Therefore, some Christian women struggle in their relationship with the Lord. They wonder why in their many years of salvation they haven't seen their marriages improve; children behave, career take off, ministry develop, their credibility established or any of the other awesome things God has promised. While they see others experience the consistent manifestation of the promises of God. When we obey His promises, we automatically choose life.

Deut 30:15-19

See, I have set before thee this day life and good, and death and evil; In that I command thee this day to love the LORD thy God, to walk in his ways, and to keep his commandments and his statutes and his judgments, that thou mayest live and multiply: and the LORD thy God shall bless thee in the land whither thou goest to possess it.

But if thine heart turn away, so that thou wilt not hear, but shalt be drawn away, and worship other gods, and serve them; I denounce unto you this day, that ye shall surely perish, and that ye shall not prolong your days upon the land, whither thou passest over Jordan to go to possess it.

I call heaven and earth to record this day against you, that I have set before you life and death, blessing and cursing: therefore choose life, that both thou and thy seed may live:

In the context of this passage of scripture, Moses had just given the Israelites the Word of God, some Holy information. Now, God tells them that they must make a choice as to whether or not they are going to obey it. The word life comes from a Word that means promise. So what God is telling us is that once we gain some biblical information, we must choose to walk in it, so that we can obtain the promise that he has for us that is associated with it.

With this in mind, I am going to give you some biblical information about the wise woman and the foolish woman. I will show you what the Word says about both of them and I will give you a God inspired, Word-aligned picture of what they look like. Once you have been exposed to them, you must choose who you will ultimately become.

PART 2

FOOLISHNESS @ WORK

WORLDLY WISDOM: THE GREAT IMPOSTER

God is such a powerful God. The Bible tells us in Psalm 147:5 that He is powerful and His understanding is infinite. His capacity of intelligence and his breadth of knowledge never end. With that never-ending knowledge, God built the universe. The Wisdom of God builds!

Yet there is another kind of wisdom that doesn't come from God, but is destructive in nature.

James 3:14-16
> *But if ye have bitter envying and strife in your hearts, glory not, and lie not against the truth. This wisdom descendeth not from above, but is earthly, sensual, and devilish. For where envying and strife is, there is confusion and every evil work.*

There are several key things to grasp from this scripture:

1. There is a wisdom that is earthly, which simply means that it exists upon and is found in the earth.
2. This wisdom consists of a limited scope of knowledge based upon the senses and human limitations.

3. This wisdom proceeds from the devil and his evil ministering
    spirits.

The wisdom that exists on this earth, in this world, is what we
call worldly wisdom. It doesn't exist in heaven, only on earth. This
is important to grasp. God makes a point of telling us that he
doesn't function like this. This is not his method or way of doing
things. It is so imperfect; it can't stand in the presence of our God.
It is the method by which the world chooses to operate.

Unlike the infinite wisdom of God, this earthly wisdom is
confined by the natural realm (the senses). It has derived out of and
is driven by the emotions, desires, whims, fancies, aversions, affec-
tions, and fleshly impulses of those who walk in it. Those who
choose to walk in this type of wisdom will be led by their flesh and
not the Spirit of God.

Galatians 5:16
>   *This I say then, Walk in the Spirit, and ye shall not*
>   *fulfill the lust of the flesh.*

Above all, this wisdom is of the devil. It proceeds from evil ministering spirits sent to lie in an attempt to steal, kill, or destroy the truth
in a person's life. Contrary to the divine character of God, this wisdom
carries all of the characteristics of the father of lies: rebellion, envy,
rivalry, jealousy, contention, provoking, wrangling, warped mentality,
irrational thinking, and blind perception/self deception (seeing things
that aren't really there/assuming stuff that isn't true).

Worldly wisdom is an impostor in the kingdom of God. It is
driven by appetites, passions and lusts of the flesh. Unfortunately,
many carnal Christians choose to walk in the natural, abandon their
faith, and tend to be deceived by this imposter. Functioning under
the influence of worldly wisdom will not net the Believer a godly
home, but will actually destroy it.

PLAYING THE FOOL
Fools, Foolishness & Folly
Everyone is familiar with the word fool. It is such a commonly

used word that it has lost its stigma over time. Nowadays, some people even use the term as a greeting or in colloquial or slang talk (i.e.: What's up fool?). However, in Bible Times, to call someone a fool was highly offensive and inappropriate. It meant that you considered them to be godless, vile, stupid, ignorant, arrogant, perverse, and mischievous, just to name a few.

Calling someone such a name, was the equivalent of speaking death over them or cursing them. This derogatory statement was so inappropriate that Matthew 5:22 says this as it relates to a brother or sister:

> *But I say unto you, That whosoever is angry with his brother without a cause shall be in danger of the judgment: and whosoever shall say to his brother, Raca, shall be in danger of the council: but whosoever shall say, Thou fool, shall be in danger of hell fire.*

Based upon the Word, we don't have the right to call someone a total fool. God is the only Supreme Being that can look down the life line of a human being, know the choices that he or she will ultimately make over the course of a lifetime and determine that based upon the Word of God and their rejection of it - they haven chosen to become a fool.

We can choose the path of the fool or we can choose to walk as a wise woman of God. Since we have a choice in the matter, God explicitly illustrates the actions of both the wise and the foolish. With these clear distinctions (that are often paralleled in Proverbs), we can make a biblically informed decision on which lifestyle we desire to lead. By displaying both lifestyles repetitiously throughout proverbs, parables and in principle, God intends for us to avoid acting like a fool.

Though there are times in a Believer's walk where he/she will do something foolish, it is not God's purpose for us to walk in foolishness and ultimately act like a fool. However, some of God's people choose to do so anyway. One Biblical account demonstrates this very thing.

The Bible tells us that Saul (who even David recognized as

anointed) tried to kill David on several accounts out of jealousy, yet later apologized to David for "playing the fool" (acting like a fool). Saul clearly knew the ways of a fool or he wouldn't have said that he was acting like one.

Folly By Default

Proverbs 22:15
> *Foolishness is bound in the heart of a child . . . .*

Proverbs 14:18
> *The simple inherit folly: but the prudent are crowned with knowledge.*

In both of these scriptures, the words folly and foolishness are the same word "ivveleth" in Hebrew. Ivveleth means stupid, silly, simple or naïve and actually has its origins in the word eviyl (which means wicked, evil). Just about anywhere you see the words wicked or evil in the Bible, you can interchange them with the word "foolish". In light of this information, there are at least two truths that God revealed to me.

- Immature Believers are inclined to be persuaded by the wisdom of the world
- If wisdom is not heeded by the Believer, Folly is exhibited by default

Worldly Persuasion
Childhood is one of the stages of progression toward adulthood. During this time in life, parents teach their children right from wrong, what's acceptable and what's not. One of the primary lessons that children learn early in life are methods or ways to stay safe or to keep away from danger. They are taught not to talk to or take anything from people they don't know; not to let people in the house if they are alone and not to touch hot things. If they aren't trained to avoid danger, they will fall into it because they are gullible. Their minds are simple. They believe almost anything that you tell them.

Similarly, when we were babes (or immature) in Christ, we were gullible to a certain extent. We were just beginning to learn what God desired of us and we didn't know how to walk in the Word in every area of our lives. This growth period was so crucial in our spiritual development, that God placed others around us, at church, school, or on the job to help us in our walk. He put pastors, teachers, and ministers in our midst to minister the Word.

All of these things were God's way of helping us, so that we wouldn't be easily persuaded to do things according to the way we did before we came to serve the Lord. God knew that if we weren't exposed to His Word, so that we had a godly choice, we would go back to operating out of the wisdom (expertise) of the world.

If wisdom is not heeded, Folly is exhibited by default

Well, what about the Believer who says in her heart that not only is there a God, but I want him to be my Lord. So she confesses him as Lord and gets saved. Then, she goes out from the church and lives an ok life. She is not doing awfully, but she's not living a victorious lifestyle either. She has sat under the Word of God for years, yet it seems as if she hasn't changed much. She continues to do the silly things that she did before. She keeps getting caught up with the same crowd she hung with before. The only thing that is different is that she attends church.

Is she saved? Is she a fool? The answer to the first question is yes, she is saved if she did according to Romans 10:9. The answer to the second question is no. She believes and has confessed God. It is the fool who says in her heart that there is no God.

So why is she acting like a fool? Well, the Believer must choose to walk in the Word of God - Neglecting to do so will result in a lifestyle of foolishness. A Christian woman, who doesn't get in her Word to: read it, meditate it, pray for revelation concerning it, and then act upon it - has made her choice. She has chosen to neglect the wisdom of God and by default has chosen to operate with the wisdom of the world - which is foolishness to God.

If she doesn't renew her mind, she will not grow and mature in the things of God. Instead, she will act as an immature babe, who will easily fall into mischief, sin, and the world's way of doing things. Though she is not a fool, she will act like one.

1 Corinthians 3:19
> *For the wisdom of this world is foolishness with God. For it is written, He taketh the wise in their own craftiness.*

EXCERPTS FROM THE LIVES OF FOOLISH WOMEN

Queen Vashti - Esther 1& 2

The queen's husband was a thoughtful, considerate, powerful, and loving man who reigned over 127 provinces from India to Ethiopia. After serving 3 years as king, we see evidence of his character when he holds a 180 day celebration and feast (basically an appreciation dinner) for all of the princes, nobles, and governors that were under his command. When that was over, the Bible says that he held another feast for all who lived in his city. He invited the most distinguished guests to those considered most insignificant.

Vashti probably had everything a wife could want: fine clothing, royal jewelry, authority, power, and most of all a husband who loved and admired her greatly. However Vashti was a foolish woman. At the last feast, he asked his servants to get Queen Vashti. He wanted her to have the royal crown on, so that the guests could see her beauty as well as her power/authority. However, she refused to come.

Vashti was foolish. Her refusal to obey her husband's request destroyed her marriage and had the potential to destroy other marriages by planting seeds of rebellion in women throughout all 127 provinces.

Lot's wife - Genesis 19

Lot was a greedy, self-centered, slothful, and compromising man. Of all of the cities he could live in, he chose to live near the most sinful people on the earth at the time. The people's wickedness kindled God's anger and he planned to destroy the city and its entire people with fire.

However God had mercy on Lot because of his covenant with

Abraham and he spared him and his family from death. The Angels told Lot where to go for safety, and not to look back once he was out of the city, but Lot lingered around Sodom. Then he asked the angels if he could flee to a small city, instead of the mountains and they were merciful. They let him go there, but they told him to hurry, because they couldn't destroy Sodom until he and his family were in a safe place.

Yet with all of this deliverance taking place, Lot's wife was foolish. Even though she was being delivered from the death and destruction that was due to the wicked, she decided to look back. Her heart was there. Her past meant so much to her, that she lost her life and family because of it.

Jezebel - 2 Kings

Jezebel was an unbeliever, who had an opportunity to let the power of God change her life. But foolishness ran rampant in her heart. She was controlling, a manipulator; and an idolater. Her decree to kill the prophets of the Lord displayed her hatred toward the people and principles of God.

Yet in the midst of her opposition toward godliness, she hired a godly man (Obadiah) to govern their home. The Bible tells us that he feared the Lord from his youth. While in Jezebel's home, Obadiah kept his relationship with the Lord and his integrity in tact while working within her ungodly household.

Even though God watched over Obadiah and kept him from her murderous reach, she didn't allow his strong commitment to the Lord, or his lack of compromise influence her iron will and rebelliousness nature. Never expressing a desire to forsake her gods for Obadiah's God, she continued to rebel against the Lord and tore her house down in the process. Ultimately, she did what she wanted to do. She lived by impulse and desire and let her flesh have its way.

Galatians 6:8

> *For he that soweth to his flesh shall of the flesh reap corruption; but he that soweth to the Spirit shall of the Spirit reap life everlasting.*

THE WRECKING CREW
Quiet Rebellion & Gentle Manipulation

Philippians 2:13

> *For it is God who works in you both **to will and to do**
> for His good pleasure.*

Ultimately, it's like God is saying to us - *Don't be fooled. It is me who enables you to accomplish My will by My spirit. Now you are able to want what I want and do as I will. I am the one who drives you to want and accomplish my purpose, so that I will be pleased. When you choose My way, I will empower you to success-fully achieve My plan.*

Just as God actively works in us, the enemy wants to actively thwart the destiny that God has for us. For that reason, it is safe to say that the opposite of this scripture is true as well: ***It is the enemy who tries to work in us both to will and do for his wicked pleasure.***

Romans 8:7

> *Because the **carnal mind** is enmity against God; for
> it is not subject to the law of God, nor indeed can be.*

One enemy the Bible clearly depicts is the carnal mind, or the flesh. The Word says the carnal mind/flesh hates the things of God and it won't submit to or follow his way. The flesh is the part of us that won't let go of superstitions, old wives tales, and ungodly advice and counsel. It is the part of us that won't readily accept what the Word says about us and our lives. It has been conditioned to do as the world has said is best to do. Carnal minded Christians are poised for failure because the flesh can't build, it can only destroy.

Let's Get Personal: My Flesh Was My Enemy
Previously, I told about how I had set ultimatums in the earlier years of my marriage. During this time I was deceived because I actually thought that doing so wouldn't harm our relationship, but strengthen it by setting boundaries and better establishing our roles. So as I rationalized my plan of execution, **my** will became more

defined and I became more determined to accomplish it.

The world conditioned me to compete with male authority. My flesh told me that anything he (a man) could do, I could do better. My flesh also persuaded me to believe that my position, status, and basic role in life was more significant than that of any male.

I could expect to have what they (men) have and more. After all, I rationalized, I deserved it because they (men) owe us for the oppressive attitudes and behaviors that they have exhibited toward women for decades - even though I wasn't necessarily one of them.

My flesh was on a rampage. Though these carnal sayings were generally toward men, now I had one and he was my husband. By default, he became the all encompassing male that my flesh wanted to fight and dominate. My flesh convinced me that my husband was the enemy to my accomplishments, successes in life and progression toward greatness.

I didn't realize it until later, but I was double-minded. I had the world influencing my flesh and the Spirit of God giving me Truth. I was too busy letting the media, unwise counsel and misperceptions poison me with lies. When things weren't functioning in our home the way that I thought they ought to, I heard the ungodly counsel loud and clear: *Don't let him run you. You need to go on and handle it, if he's going to act like that. You don't need him, he needs you. You need to show him a thing or two. He doesn't know what he's doing anyway. He thinks you are stupid. Who does he think you are?*

But when I listened to the wisdom of God's Word, I knew that my husband, a son of the Most High God, had the spirit of God driving him to do and to want God's will for his life. God wanted his best for me, so the Spirit of God had to tell my husband to desire God's best for me too.

As a Believer, I had the Spirit of God inside of me, yet I had carnal thoughts running things in the marriage department. I allowed my flesh to encourage my will and then I acted out. If I hadn't let the Lord intercept my plan, there were two things that I would have inevitably done to destroy my marriage: ***rebel and manipulate***.

The Bible likens rebellion as the sin of witchcraft. Witchcraft is a sin because it involves idolatry and God tells us to have no other gods before him. Therefore, being rebellious is like witchcraft because when a person rebels, they elevate themselves above the authority that God has established and have esteemed themselves as the authority.

My flesh, that part of me that wanted its way, began to devise a strategy. Now it wasn't a detailed strategy, it was actually quite simple. First, I wasn't going to let him be my head, like the Word said he was. Oftentimes, I would obey or meet his needs when I felt that he appreciated it. I even agreed with him on many issues, but I defied his authority. In other words, I didn't actually revere him as the head of the household and I refused to fully submit to him.

He could've quoted a zillion scriptures, but his influence wasn't going to outweigh the weight of my will. Second, if I removed some things from my husband's life that I knew he wanted from me, then I could hold those things like hostages until I got what I wanted.

No matter how I planned to execute it, my strategy wouldn't work unless I employed it. Like a car with a fresh tank of gas, I was ready to roll. Fleshly thoughts mixed with carnal wisdom became a catalyst for me to do as I willed. I had to stand up to him and I couldn't fold. I had to let him know that I wore the pants just as much as he did. So, I began to will and to do as it pleased my flesh.

Unknowingly, I created a path of destruction to my house by halting his ability to function as the head of our household. It was as if I tied his hands behind his back. When he needed to make decisions, not only did I give my input, but I expected for him to always agree with me.

When he didn't, my flesh rose up. I quietly tortured him by not washing his clothes, refusing to cook the things that I knew he liked, not being romantic with him, and withholding due benevolence.

Just to show you how spiritually ignorant I was, I did all of these things while I prayed for the Lord to help our marriage. It truly was the Spirit of God in me asking the Lord to help us, so He would be pleased.

Even though it only lasted for nearly a year, I became tired of this way of life. I continued to pray for help until God fully manifested all of the help that I needed. First, He began to show me the state that I was in and where my flesh would take me if I continued to walk in it. Then, he gave me a clear picture of what a foolish woman looked like according to the Word.

THE FULL ARMOR OF THE WORLD

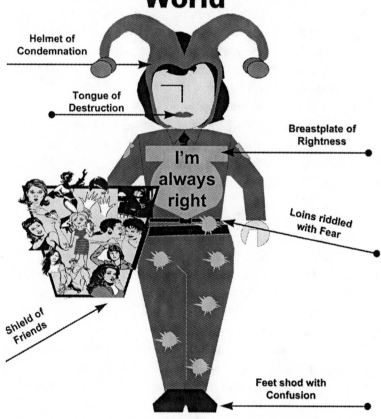

The Foolish Woman in The Full Armor of the World

Helmet of Condemnation

Tongue of Destruction

Breastplate of Rightness

I'm always right

Loins riddled with Fear

Shield of Friends

Feet shod with Confusion

Note: This woman depicts the folly that even a Believer will exhibit if she doesn't walk in the wisdom of the Lord.

Heart of Domination
Proverbs 28:26 (Amplified)

> *He who leans on, trusts in, and is confident of his own mind and heart is a [self-confident] fool, but he who walks in skillful and godly wisdom shall be delivered.*

The foolish woman is led by her mind and her heart. Think of it this way, her unrenewed mind is like an athlete who wants to win, her heart is the best friend who thinks that she knows everything, and the Holy Spirit is the coach who sees her true purpose and desires to lead her to fulfill it.

Now, this is the deal. The Holy Spirit knows exactly what she can accomplish and he is willing to guide her to victory if she will just do what he says to do. He has the plan that will cause her to go forth with great peace, strength, endurance, and glory. His reason for being is so that she will succeed in life.

On the other hand, her heart tells her what she wants to hear. If she doesn't want to train, she doesn't have to. If she doesn't want to change her routine, she doesn't have to. Her heart doesn't know what will cause her to have victory. It is like the best friend who knows a little bit about the sport, but doesn't know how to win.

So, when the foolish woman hears what the Holy Spirit says she has to do in order to win, she doesn't think that it takes all of that. At this point, she places her mind under no obligation to submit to Him. She has already made her choice. She would rather listen to her heart who promises her victories she doesn't know how to get, rather than seize the opportunity to have the Ultimate Coach transform her life.

Ecclesiastes 10:2 (Amplified)

> *A wise man's heart turns him toward his right hand, but a fool's heart toward his left.*

The right hand signifies the favor and authority of the Lord. A person who allows the Word to bring wisdom will obtain the favor and the authority (power) of the Lord. But a foolish woman's heart will drive her away from his favor and power. As with most peer pressure, her heart coach has flattered her for so long, she is willing to listen to whatever it has to say and do whatever it wants her to do.

For years it has lured her with false assurances of victory, illusions of self-confidence, and notions of godless independence. Now, it will convince her to do the opposite of what the Holy Spirit instructs her to do.

Even though the coach knows the winning plan that God has for her life and is ready to give instruction in line with her destiny. But she won't hear Him. She'd rather be led by her heart, whose primary goal is to give her instantaneous results, no matter how temporary they may be. As a result, she may think she's ok, but she will never experience her full potential as a Believer.

Helmet of Condemnation

Romans 13:1, 2 (NASB)
> *Let every person be in subjection to the governing authorities. For there is no authority except from God, and those which exist are established by God. Therefore he who resists authority has opposed the ordinance of God; and they who have opposed will receive condemnation upon themselves.*

God has set up a system of divine order. Within this system, he has set in place positions of authority. The scripture above tells us 5 things about this authority:

- Everyone is to submit to governing authorities as unto the Lord.
  (spousal, ministerial, executive, management, supervisory, administrative)

- There is no authority given except by God
  (The authority doesn't reside within the person, but within the position God has established)

- Those in positions of authority were put there by God

- If we resist God's authority, we have opposed his commandment (to submit).

- Once we oppose God's authority, we have opposed him, and we invite condemnation to come upon us.

God, in his sovereignty, places people in positions of authority. Whether they are elected, hired, volunteer, or inherit these positions. Therefore, he commands that everyone submit (willingly obey) the rules, codes, regulations, procedures, policies established and enforced by them.

From the start, the foolish woman opposes this commandment. She obeys on her own terms and establishes her own system of order which goes something like this: There are rules and regulations in every arena of life. However, if any of the people who are enforcing them offends disrespects, gets an attitude or is simply someone she just "doesn't like" - she doesn't have to follow the rules any longer.

At this point, she neither understands nor cares about authority. She believes she doesn't have to bend for anyone. She disregards the fact that God has set these people in places of authority that she must interface with on a regular basis, whether mature or immature, saved or unsaved.

Instead, she takes offense, allows the offenses to distract her from the truth (God's commandment to submit as unto Him), and objects to the rules and laws that govern her. She rationalizes why she doesn't need to pay tithes, she rationalizes why her employer deserves a piece of her mind, she rationalizes why she doesn't have to give all of her financial information on her taxes, she even rationalizes why she needs to park in the handicapped spot in the church parking lot (when she really isn't physically challenged).

Her ridiculous reasons why she shouldn't have or need to obey the laws that have been established and her explanation of how inept those in authority are dominate her conversation. Pastors, ministry workers, ushers, hotel managers, supermarket cashiers, department store clerks, librarians, teachers, school administrators, and policeman have a hard time with this woman.

Proverbs 3:35
> *The wise shall inherit glory: but shame shall be the promotion of fools.*

Both the wise and foolish are compensated for their methods of handling wisdom once they have been exposed to it. The Word says that the wise (those who function with the wisdom of God) receives a crown of grace and glory, but the foolish (those who reject the wisdom of God) receives what the Bible calls the promotion of fools - shame and disgrace.

The foolish woman's compensation for opposing God's commandment to submit to those in authority - is condemnation, which is both a disgraceful and shameful punishment. When something is condemned, it has been declared unfit for use. Therefore, God can't use this woman because she has disqualified herself by disobedience and lack of submission to authority.

Unlike the glistening, radiant, and vibrant jewels of a crown, the foolish woman dons something that probably looks like a jester's hat in the spirit. Drab, droopy, and foolish looking, this headpiece says:

- I am strong-willed and ignorant
- Submission is conditional, I do it when I feel like it
- I have no clue that when I submit to authority; God says that I am actually submitting to him
- Though I consider myself to be a Believer, right now I am disobedient and temporarily unfit for God's use

Romans 8:1 (Amplified)
> *Therefore, [there is] now no condemnation (no adjudging guilty of wrong) for those who are in Christ Jesus, who live [and] walk not after the dictates of the flesh, but after the dictates of the Spirit.*

Note: The Bible tells us that not every authority that we are commanded to submit to is righteous, nor is every one of them mature. That is why he tells us that it is all unto HIM anyway. Our eyes must not focus on the person's inconsistencies, inadequacies, failures, ignorance, ungodliness, or offensive behavior, etc. If what we are obeying or following doesn't defile our temples and isn't full of wickedness or evil, we are required by God to comply.

1 Peter 2:18
> *Servants, be subject to your masters with all fear; not only to the good and gentle, but also to the froward.*

Tongue of Destruction

Proverbs 14:9 (Amplified)
> *Fools make a mock of sin and sin mocks the fools [who are its victims; a sin offering made by them only mocks them, bringing them disappointment and disfavor], but among the upright there is the favor of God.*

The mouth of the foolish woman is like the forked tongue on a king cobra snake. There is a schism in the way she chooses to communicate. Sometimes she will rely upon the Word of God to direct her mouth and other times she will rely upon her feelings to direct her mouth. There is no consistency, just double-talk.

On the one hand she knows that she must live a lifestyle that is pleasing to God, yet when she observes sin - she jokes about it. In other words, she takes it lightly almost as if willing to commit the sin herself. Eventually she may fall into the same sin she humored, which will compound the shame that she already wears from being disobedient and unsubmitted to God's commandments.

This woman's heart has coached her to do and say things contrary to the Word of God. Since she has chosen to trust in her heart and not in the wisdom of God, she is vulnerable to use her mouth to murmur, complain, nag, gossip, backbite, exaggerate, lie, slander, gripe, whine and criticize.

Totally unrestrained by the wisdom in self-control, she is loud and quick to give someone a piece of her mind. Her sarcastic and sometimes hostile comments to the restaurant server who makes a mistake on her bill; her harsh crowd-drawing words toward a store manager who won't let her return an item that's past the date of return; her back-biting comments about her teacher who gave her the grade she actually earned; and her insensitive and hurtful remarks toward her stressed husband (who she thinks ought to sit down and give her the reins) say to all that she is foolish.

Ecclesiastes 10:3 (Amplified)
> *Even when he who is a fool walks along the road, his heart and understanding fail him, and he says of everyone and to everyone that he is a fool.*

She ignorantly misleads others by counseling them according to the worldly knowledge she has trusted and relied upon - and that has failed her time and time again. As a result, those who habitually listen to her and those who habitually follow her will eventually fall into similar mistakes, mishaps, and pitfalls of the foolish woman.

Proverbs 14:7 (Amplified)
> *Go from the presence of a foolish and self-confident man, for you will not find knowledge on his lips.*

Constantly upset that things aren't going the way that she wants them to (in her life), she doesn't make the connection that the daily victories she longs for will not become a regular occurrence until she speaks and depends upon and walks in the Word and wisdom of God.

Breastplate of Rightness

Proverbs 18:2 (Amplified)
> *A [self-confident] fool has no delight in understanding but only in revealing his personal opinions and himself.*

The foolish woman has a lot to say. An authority on what seems like every subject known to man, she believes that has either heard it, seen it, or done it before in her lifetime. With a trick bag full of hypothetical situations, she has watched the day time talk shows and many of the soap operas at some point in her lifetime. She has made mental notes of the testimonies, examples, clinical counsel, television counsel, and unwise counsel that was given over the airwaves. Sometimes she even correctly guessed some of the answers and counsel that these trained, untrained and unwise people gave.

As a result, she believes that she is equipped and has expertise in handling situations and solving problems - because she gave some of the same television counsel to her friends and it temporarily worked. Now her girl friends look to her as the one who has the answers, the mature one. So, she sticks her chest out, as if to say, you need to listen to me. It is almost as if there is an invisible breastplate that reads, I TOLD YOU and I KNOW in big bold letters.

In addition, this is a woman who has been exposed to the life-changing Word of God over a course of months, years or even decades, but she doesn't trust in the Lord. She hears what God has for her, but she doesn't believe that he will do it for her. She hears the Word, contemplates its relevancy to her life, as she ultimately decides whether she will walk in it or not.

In her ignorance, she fails to understand that God's wisdom is manifold. God has an infinite expression of wisdom from which a specific and divine plan for her life is waiting to be revealed. But she won't go to the Lord for his plan; she wants to do what she wants to do. One minute, she thinks that "it doesn't take all of that" when it comes to disciplining herself to follow the wisdom of the Lord. The next minute she thinks, "That's too easy, it must be something more".

Finally, using herself as an escape goat, she rationalizes and assumes that she knows enough to get herself through any situation or challenge in life. She figures that she knows best. "If things don't work out, she reasons, at least I can't blame it on God - I don't have anyone to blame but myself."

Having stored what she considers wisdom over the course of her lifetime, she strives to attain honor from those who ask for her opinions. But it's all vanity. She will never receive the honor that comes from walking in the wisdom of the Word of God. The wisdom of the world is foolishness to God.

Proverbs 12:15 (Amplified)
The way of a fool is right in his own eyes, but he who listens to counsel is wise.

Loins riddled with Fear

Proverbs 28:1 (Amplified)
The wicked flee when no man pursues them, but the [uncompromisingly] righteous are bold as a lion.

The foolish woman hides behind the Breastplate of Rightness, yet she is full of fear. Truthfully, she is uneasy about her decisions, her opinions, her own counsel and her future. By choosing to disobey the wisdom of God and follow her own way, she has disqualified herself from receiving a consistent flow of God's grace in her life. She can't walk in the boldness of the righteous, because she hasn't done what is "right" in the sight of God. She has chosen her own way (disobedience), and instead she gives way to fear.

She may not necessarily experience the immediate hair-raising dread or terror of the horror movie queen, but her encounter with fear is long-lasting. Yet she encounters a subtle gnawing fear that, like a time-released capsule, slowly penetrates every area of her life. This fear comes in the way of insecurity. She doesn't feel secure. There is no certainty with her.

When she looks at other Believers who walk in the wisdom of God, she begins to feel inadequate as she gives way to another type of fear, paranoia. This paranoia exists in the form of the "I got to watch my back" mentality.

The foolish woman's thinking is distracted by others - Believers and non-believers alike. When she sees Believers prospering in their walk with the Lord or when the ungodly appear to be successful, she reflects upon her own life. Soon after, she begins to think that others are the reason for her demise, others are persecuting her and holding her back, and others are trying to set her up.

So, in a spirit of competition, she lives a defensive lifestyle, always bragging about how well she is doing (rarely giving honor or praise to the Lord) as she competes for the success that she sees the wise women walking in. In this state, the foolish woman has an intense fear that no matter what her endeavors are, they probably won't work out. Therefore, her actions lead to another form of fear, anxiety. Unlike the wise woman who has faith, believing those things that she can't see with her natural eyes, the foolish woman is anxious and worrisome.

She only believes things that she can see and what she often sees are immovable obstacles along her path, so she worries about heading in that direction. The very thing that she wants, she is afraid to have. Her expectation for success has been soured by fear. She wants to succeed, but she is really afraid to. She feels that she can't get the new job assignment, she can't teach her children, she can't minister to her family - and she is absolutely right.

She can't effectively do any of these things if she continues to reject the wisdom of God, because anxiety, insecurity and para-noia will zap her strength and tear through her like a bullet through a target.

Sadly, the constant worry and anxiety drives her to experience the fear of evil. She watches the news and begins to make extraordi-nary precautions to protect herself from the armed robber who escaped from the penitentiary 3 states away from her. She is over-protective of her material belongings thinking that someone may steal them at any time.

She has alarms, latches, pad-locks, peepholes, burglar bars, and iron doors on her house, not to mention her car. She is like a pris-oner in her own environment. She carries a knife, mace, a baseball bat, and a gun. She doesn't feel safe. She sends and forwards numerous emails to all of her friends about the perils of society. Since she thinks that she has everything under control, she has chosen not to rely upon the Word that says that when the Lord is her Shepherd, she does not have to fear because God will protect her.

At times, even the insecurity gets the best of her. Then she begins to have "bad dreams", nightmares. She can't sleep at night because the fear comes over her like a chilling blanket. She hides from under her covers, afraid to look to the left or to the right because she may encounter a gruesome situation. Much of this anxiety, paranoia, and insecurity exist because she didn't accept and walk in the wisdom of the Lord.

Proverbs 3:21, 24

> *My son, let not them depart from thine eyes: keep sound wisdom and discretion: When thou liest down, thou shalt not be afraid: yea, thou shalt lie down, and thy sleep shall be sweet.*

Shield of Friends

Proverbs 27:12 (Amplified)

> *A prudent man sees evil and hides himself, but the simple pass on and are punished [with suffering].*

The foolish woman has many "girl friends", buddies or best friends. Not "sisters" or "brothers" in the Lord, who will pray with her and for her, exhort her to do God's word, and love her unconditionally. She doesn't surround herself with wise women who refuse to half-step, straddle the fence, or live lives without godly compromise.

The wise women who aren't hanging out in the streets, going to every party, every sale, every main attraction, bore the foolish woman. If she were to spend her time with them, she rationalizes; she would be living like an old lady. So instead, she opts to hang with compromising or flat out ungodly women.

A group that likes to laugh at foolish things, talk about others faults, complain about injustices, slander those who have offended them, spread others business, rejoice in others downfalls, and even turn their noses up at others who have a tangible manifestation of the Lord's blessing on their lives. She feels more comfortable with this group. These women don't have the conviction of the Holy Spirit urging them toward the truth of God's word. Instead, they have a lack of wisdom and reliance upon listening to their heart (feelings) that urges them toward things that please their flesh.

Some of them even say, "You've got to go with your feelings girl."

Ecclesiastes 7:4 (NASB)
> *The heart of the wise is in the house of mourning,*
> *but the heart of fools is in the house of mirth and*
> *sensual joy.*

The wise woman's heart is in the house of mourning. In other words, when she hears the Word of God, she allows it to minister to her. She realizes where she missed it, made some mistakes or traveled down a self-created (not God directed) path, then she grasps and then walks in the Word necessary in order to avoid those same mistakes. But the foolish woman's heart is in the house of mirth and sensual joy.

Mirth is uncontrollable laughter at the outbreak of something ridiculous. When people do things to ridicule others or themselves, it amuses her. In other words when people, slip on a shoestring and fall wildly on their bottoms, play mindless practical jokes on one another, or dog each other in sitcom dialogue, she thinks that it is funny. Fat jokes, jokes that make light of others stupidity, racial jokes, and tasteless political jokes all cause her to laugh. Anything "naughty" is bound to make her at least chuckle.

Her heart is in the house of sensual joy. She has been told and firmly believes that she's got to have "fun" 24-7 (i.e.: She has to do things, say things, eat things and even buy things that bring immediate satisfaction to herself). Since she is ignorant to the Word, she doesn't know that she can delight herself in the Lord and then he will give her the desires of her heart. Neither does she understand that God is no respecter of persons.

So if the foolish woman will get some wisdom and begin to obey the Word, she can have the blessings and promises associated with it. She doesn't have to dog others for what she hasn't positioned herself for God to do in her life. Yet, her ignorance consistently places her in situations and with people that she has no business being around. The foolish woman is often caught up in, tied to, involved with - "some mess"! Do you know what I mean? She always has "drama" going on in her life and around her life.

This woman is headed for disaster. She listens to what her friends say, and then acts like she already knows what to do. When in actuality, she receives their advice and words like a wise woman receives the counsel of the Lord. She adheres to her friends' advice and words, and she errs greatly. She may treat someone disrespectfully, think of someone poorly, or even speak of someone slanderously based upon the false information that she received and then believed.

Her "friends", who are only out for themselves, may set her up for their own self gain. Using the phone as a vice, they try to get her to say things about others who quietly wait on the other line ready to bust her, and the end result is mess. Thus, she causes herself to gain enemies, a poor reputation, and become a disgrace in the sight of God.

There is nothing wrong with having many righteous brothers and sisters in the Lord, but when the foolish woman is surrounded by "friends" who are not Believers, she is headed for a fall.

Proverbs 18:24a (NASB)
> *A man of many friends comes to ruin.*
> ***Feet shod with Confusion***

Proverbs 19:3 (Amplified)
> *The foolishness of man subverts his way [ruins his affairs]; then his heart is resentful and frets against the Lord.*

The wise woman esteems God's word as a lamp to her feet and a light to her path. She relies upon it to give her direction, exhortation, and encouragement and wisdom. As she builds her relationship with him (through prayer, obedience), he provides practical ways that she can consistently progress down the path of (abundant) life. However, it isn't so with the foolish woman.

The foolish woman subverts (defeats) her way. She tries to beat the system. She wants to walk the path of abundant life, but without godly wisdom. She has an expectation to be blessed as the daughter of the Lord, but trading human wisdom (what she has gathered from trial and error) for her Father's wisdom spiritually blinds her. So she tries secretly and desperately to find her way to the path of (abundant) life, but she is in the dark.

Proverbs 1:32 (NASB)
*For the waywardness of the naïve shall kill them,
and the complacency of fools shall destroy them.*

There are only 2 gates. One is straight and narrow and leads to the fullness of life and the other is broad and leads to destruction. When the foolish woman raises up her shield of friends or follows her flesh, (so that she remains ignorant to the things of God) she opts for the broad gate - which will ultimately destroy or kill her.

Waywardness is the act of walking away from the path that God has led you to and walking down the path that you have chosen. Her heart tells her that if she walks her self-directed path she can make it in life without doing all of the stuff that the Word says to do. Yet she is deceived because her path is dark. It has no wisdom or light.

She has truly put herself in a predicament that she must get out of if she is going to live a pleasing life to the Lord. Just think, this whole thing started when she decided to disobey the commandments of the Lord and refuse to submit to his will, lowering upon her head the Helmet of Condemnation. As the shame of disobedience riddled her Loins with Fear, its cohorts (uncertainty, apprehension and insecurity) became a preeminent part of her life.

Then, her Tongue of Destruction spewed false contentment with her lifestyle, the vanity of doing things God's way, and her unstable thoughts about the Word and wisdom of God.

Yet in order to camouflage her fear her Dominating Heart convinced her that in conjunction with her Shield of Friends, they could lead her to victory. So, while she thinks that she is progressing in life, her Feet are covered with Confusion. She is bruised and beaten up from her falls, doesn't know which way to turn, and her way is dark.

In her ignorance and confusion, she doesn't see her consistent disobedience and her failure to receive godly wisdom, all she sees is that she is in trouble and she can't find God. "I am a child of God," she cries. "This isn't supposed to happen to me" she wails. She begins to ponder that God could've stepped in and kept her from falling. God could've prevented her from the hurts and pains of doing things her own way. God could've told her that what she did would hurt and could eventually destroy her.

The foolish woman is totally confused. She just doesn't get it. She holds resentment, anger, bitterness in her heart toward God for her own mistakes. She followed her own way, relied upon herself, and she blames God. Her heart deceived her into thinking that by following her own way; she could progress toward a life that is only designated for those seeking the wisdom of God.

Proverbs 4:26 (Amplified)
> *Consider well the path of your feet, and let all your ways be established and ordered aright.*

7 CARNAL BELIEFS THAT CAN WRECK A HOUSEHOLD

A carnal belief develops when a person relies upon and regards worldly wisdom like it is the Word. Remember, God clearly tells us that the wisdom of the world is foolishness to him. Therefore carnal beliefs are foolish. They have some truth in them, yet they are primarily distorted truths, therefore a lie.

Merely hearing a lie will not destroy your life, but believing them can. Lies have destructive potential for 3 reasons: they bring strife, a resistant attitude toward the truth, and disobedience. We see evidence of this in the Garden of Eden.

Carnality & the First Couple

The first couple believed that they could be like God if they did what the serpent told them to do. The serpent persuaded them with his craftiness, distortion of truth, foolishness, that if they disobeyed God – they could be like God. The truth of the matter is that God had already created them in his image. So why would they need to disobey God in order to be like him? They were in essence, already like him.

As simply foolish as this may seem to us, Eve contemplated the lie. Next she rationalized it, then she accepted it as truth, and committed the sin of disobedience as a result.

I believe that the devil knew that if they believed the lies, they would not only be punished, but they would no longer have the privilege of living their lives in the fullness of God. If they would never have received the lies of the devil, into their hearts as truth - they wouldn't have disobeyed the Lord.

We, as believers, are admonished in 2 Corinthians not to be ignorant of the devil's devices, schemes, or plans. Sometimes, a lie is released in an atmosphere where the enemy counts on your spiritual defenses being down - like in the midst of someone telling a joke or in a situation that's designed to humor you.

When we hear jokes that demoralize, slander, criticize, or even tear down "men" "husbands" or "males", we need to stop and refer to the Word. We shouldn't even for a moment think it's cute or funny. As Believers, these things should not be acceptable or amusing to us.

Let me give you an example: While on my way home from running some errands one day, I saw a lady in her mid 30's and her very young daughter driving a relatively new van. As I drove up a little closer, I noticed a bumper sticker on the back door of the van. The bumper sticker read, GROW YOUR OWN DOPE, PLANT A MAN. I wasn't amused. This sticker wasn't on the bumper; it was right at eye level on the back of the van.

Whether the lady was godly or ungodly, that kind of lie received into the heart of a young child or adult is destined to bring strife into a marriage. It didn't matter whether her past or current male relationships were awful; God said that he created man in his image. God didn't make any dopey men. Whether her experiences said that he was a knucklehead or not, that is not what God intended for him to be. God intended for him and every other man to be a reflection of him.

As Believers, there is no time to rationalize or sympathize with carnal views. If we begin to consider and receive this information as truth and not a lie, we will eventually begin to act upon them. We will view our spouses or future spouses as stupid, uncaring, or crazy.

Carnal Beliefs and My Marriage

Early on, I began to grasp this truth concerning my marriage, I realized something quite significant. Some of the perceptions that had been sown into my life concerning marriage were lies.

Over time, I began to rationalize the things that I heard because everyone spoke about these things with such a passion and conviction as if it were the truth of God's word. Then, I began taking my personal experiences and others personal experiences and establishing them as a solid foundation of truth. After all, people consider what they have experienced to be valid.

I realized that over the course of my lifetime, the enemy strategically plotted situations in which I would hear the exact opposite of what God wanted me to believe concerning a husband or potential husband. Those lies came through the mouths of loved ones, friends, teachers and my own mind with such experience-based conviction that I believed them. The same potentially destructive devices the enemy used on me are some of the same ones that he has been releasing into the lives of women and wives for centuries.

The lies that you are about to read are not the only ways that the enemy comes to wives or single women, but they are common ways. If you believe and act upon lies like these, you will release strife, and eventually destroy your household by your own hands.

In the following chapter, I am going to take you on a journey through the life of a woman who has had lies interjected throughout her life from youth to adulthood and then marriage. In doing so, you won't be looking at the scenario from the outside in, but from the inside out. Thus, you will be able to clearly see how each carnal belief moves like the ferocious winds of a tornado, gaining momentum as it picks up the lies before it and twists them until they hit their final destination - a household ~ a family ~ a marriage.

Although these are not the life stories of one specific person or individual, she represents many of us who have been vulnerable to believe such lies.

Proverbs 14:1

> *Every wise woman buildeth her house: but the foolish plucketh it down with her hands.*

Carnal Belief #1
You can't trust men

Scenario

Aunt Sally, Cousin Josephine, and Grandma Mary are in grandma's living room. Aunt Sally is unsaved and has unsuccessfully attempted marriage 3 times. Grandma is saved and married to grandpa for nearly 50 years. Josephine just went through a separation from her husband of 12 years. She just found out that her husband had been having an affair and kept it from her for 5 years. Now Josephine is separated and she goes to Aunt Sally and Grandma Mary for some encouragement and counsel.

Aunt Sally passionately tells Josephine that you can't trust men. After all, she knows. She has had numerous ungodly relationships and none of them produced a husband. The last 3 fiancé's that she had were unfaithful to her. All they wanted was her money and the worship they thought that she could give them. Grandma tells Josephine that she knows how men can be. With her silvery gray crown of hair, creamy skin, and fine wrinkles around her wisdom filled eyes, she has seen a lot through the years. Though she loves her husband of 50 years, she says gently and convincingly ~ you can't trust men. Now your mind is ringing with the critical words "You can't trust men."

Men, she says, will do a lot of things that they don't tell you about. She experienced that hurt first hand from her husband, who happened to be her school sweetheart. She experienced the hurt of his infidelity while away serving his country in the armed services. She experienced the hurt of the lies and denial of having the affairs. But through it all, she decided to stay. She decided to hold it all together and let the Lord work it all out.

While this conversation went on Josephine cried, Aunt Sally agreed and Grandma embraced the two as you sat on the sofa in silence. At the impressionable age of 12, the critical words rang in your mind at every stage in your young life ~ you can't trust men.

Carnal Belief #2
Men just want sex

Scenario

It's Monday morning and you are sitting in class waiting for the lunch bell to ring. As it rings, you jump up out of your desk and head for the cafeteria. While waiting in line, you overhear two of your 8th grade teachers (Miss Jenkins and Miss King) talking about their weekend dating experiences. Barely out of college and with only 2 years of teaching experience in the junior high, the teachers have begun to recklessly discuss their personal business at the lunch table in front of the students.

Miss Jenkins tells her friend that her handsome boyfriend is so "frisky", but he never listens to her. "He always wants his way with me, she reflects, and I give it to him." They both begin to burst out in girlish laughter. Ms. Jenkins then says that her boyfriend of 3 months is so fine that she can't help herself. Her friend nods and laughs in agreement. Then she begins to tell her all of the things that this boyfriend buys for her. She describes some of the gifts in detail all the way down to the negligee that he bought for her on Valentine's Day.

As you eat your lunch, you notice that Ms. King, pleased with what she has heard, smiles and tells her ~ girl, all that men want sex. Then, she advises her to keep the guy as long as he continues to pamper her with "things". After this personal, yet public moment, the school bell rings and it is time to go back to class.

While going back to your desk, you notice a young man looking at you and desperately trying to get you to notice him. You contemplate doing one of two things. Either you look away in disgust thinking that he is just lustful, since all men want is sex or you decide that you are ready to give men what they want – which eventually causes you to defile your body.

Carnal Belief #3
Men are control freaks

Scenario

You have an older sister who goes to the movies with a group of her friends - 3 girls and 2 guys. She is the only one that is not paired up in the group. They are going to see a movie about a 19 year old guy who is trying to get with a 16 year old girl. Since he is older, he is thought to be wiser and her parents welcome his mature presence.

Yet in time, he exposes his jealousy toward his young girl-friend's circle of friends. Eventually, the parents of the girl disapprove of her relationship with him, noticing that their daughter is now obeying him instead of them. They warn her of his controlling and manipulative behavior on numerous occasions, fearing that his jealous outbursts and anger binges will lead to abuse.

As the movie progresses he ends up giving his young girl an ultimatum. She can't have both him and her immature friends. She must choose between the two. Bound by her lust, rebellion and false love for him, she chooses to keep her relationship with this controlling brute.

As your sister gives you this movie review, you notice that the 2 couples in her group share some similar character traits of the actors and actresses in the movie. In the past, you have heard your sister talking about how the guys use mind games and other psychological techniques to keep his girl at his beckon call; and the other one continually has the girl confess her "love" for him, without any reciprocity of the act.

After your sister's friends leave, you ask her why those guys were like that in real life and in the movie and she tells you with confidence ~ men are control freaks.

Carnal Belief #4
I need to run things (I'm in control)

Scenario

You are out of high school and on your way to college. Your goal is to finish your undergraduate studies with the highest honors possible and then attend graduate school. You want to be the first in your family to have a graduate degree and you are determined to let nothing come between you or your degrees – especially not a man. "You have to get yours" is what you have been told.

In your young life you have seen the ups and downs of boyfriend/girlfriend and husband/wife relationships. You have learned that you can't trust men because all they want is sex. You have also seen the way that guys on campus control girls. You have seen them play games like giving their girls the silent treatment, neglecting to respond to their phone calls or flattering the girls to the point of it being disgusting for others to watch. After seeing all of this, you tell yourself that you don't want a relationship while in college. As a matter of fact, you don't need a man at all!

However, while watching TV in the lobby of your freshman girl's dorm one day, a young man (who is also watching TV) attracts your attention. He is nice looking, well-dressed and very polite. After the two of you are introduced, you talk to him for a while and realize that he is intelligent, charming and even has a great sense of humor. Slowly, you begin to spend time with him. Everything will be okay you tell yourself because you will be in control.

You will make sure that you don't let him have any piece of your emotions. You will not allow him to dictate when he calls you or when he comes to visit. Instead, you will tell him when he should call and where you both will meet. If he falls short in any situation, you are determined not to let it affect or ruin your day.

As the semester progresses, you two begin a relationship, but you are determined to be ahead in the control department. You carefully and thoughtfully contribute to the relationship to the degree that you will not allow yourself to be hurt. After all, you have got to be ahead and stay "in control."

Carnal Belief #5
He acts like I'm stupid

Scenario
The guy that you met in your freshman year of college has now become your fiancé. When he proposed to you, he said that he would

be your knight in shining armor. He promised to provide for you and support you in every way possible. He cherishes your presence.

One day he invites you to his off campus apartment to cook dinner for you. He then turns the television on and is fascinated with the syndicated sitcoms channel. He begins to tell you the show schedule for the next 2 hours. The line up included shows like: All in the Family, The Jefferson's and Married with Children – none of which you think are good healthy entertainment.

At this point you realize that sometimes his idea of what is funny and entertaining doesn't line up with yours. You are fully aware that in all three of these shows, the marriage relationships are dysfunctional.

The men in the sitcoms are untrustworthy and controlling; they're always doing something behind their wives backs. When the wives find out about it, the husband is already in trouble and in need of sympathy while they dig themselves out of a hole. On the other hand, the insecure, yet independence driven wives are busy trying to establish their self-worth, while being considered objects of their husband's selfish desires.

This is not your idea of good humor. As you watch him enjoy one of these shows, a light bulb goes off in your mind. Aha! He probably thinks that this is the way that our household will run. Oh but no! "It's not going to be that way in my house", you rationalize with great intensity. He must think I'm stupid if he thinks that he's going to talk to me or treat me like they treat their wives. I am not stupid!

Carnal Belief #6
He thinks that I don't do anything all day!

Scenario
Now you two are married. Your morning routines are quite different. He gets up before you, turns on every light in the house and leaves them on as he rushes out of the door to beat morning traffic. Awake, but trying to get the last bit of rest now for nearly 45 minutes, you wake up and begin your day. Once dressed, you are on your way to a full day of graduate school classes.

Your classes end about one hour from the time he gets home.

You have just enough time to rest for at least 30 minutes before it's time to cook dinner. While the dinner is cooking, you begin to look around the house checking to make sure that everything is in order and organized. You notice mail strewn about, shoes here and there and the clothes hamper overflowing with dirty clothes. Then, you begin to start separating and washing clothes one load at a time.

By now, your husband walks in the door, gives you a kiss, tells you he loves you and sits on the sofa to vegetate for a moment. You begin telling him a little bit about your day as you set the table. It's dinner time! You call out, as he changes from his work clothes to some lounging clothes. As he makes his way to the table, he tells you about his day. Then he asks you if you got a chance to pay a couple of bills, take the shirts to be dry cleaned or pick up some apples for him from the grocery store.

"No, I was in school all day, remember?" you respond swiftly. I just got home about an hour ago. Boy, you begin to think – *He must think that I do nothing all day. Doesn't he appreciate the dinner, the clean house and laundry? I go to school all day, come home and still work. I don't get paid for the work that I do and he gets a paycheck every other week.*

Shoot! Forget our agreement. I'll keep working from home, but I am also going to go get a job. I'll work all day, so nothing gets done around here. Then maybe he'll see how valuable I am – in dollar bills. I need to get double paid for what I do. I have skills!!

Carnal Belief #7
He won't help me with the kids

Scenario
    A year passes and the two of you have decided to have a baby. You have come to the conclusion that you want to start a family and then finish graduate school. You want to have children in your youth – you are willing to make that sacrifice. You're a pretty fertile girl and he's a pretty fertile guy and your plans have now become a reality. You are pregnant.

Your husband's morning routine continues. Lights are turned on all over, drawers are left opened, shoes are left in multiple locations and cereal bowls are left on the counters, instead of in the sink. By your and your husband's prayers and your support, he gets a promotion to executive status. Now, his salary and benefits have increased tremendously.

Though this is quite awesome, it means more work for you. Now he will work late hours and begin to travel quite often – several times monthly. Sometimes he will even be required to be gone for weeks at a time to get special leadership training.

This means that you will have to anticipate nights alone in your urban located bungalow, without a security alarm. You will have to wash clothes and make trips to the dry cleaners more often, cook and eat meals alone and sleep in a cold bed while he is gone – all while you are pregnant.

Man, with him being gone like this he's not going to have time to help me with our son/daughter, you ponder while folding clothes. Is his agreement to my pregnancy rooted in a desire to control me? Maybe he thinks that I don't do anything all day and I need to be kept busy. I don't have to stay at home while I'm pregnant. I can go and get a job. I am not a housewife.

I am married to my husband, not my house. I have skills, if he doesn't appreciate them someone else will! I tell you what; our child isn't going to come into this world with a father so busy, that he only sees him at bedtime.

So I guess I'm going to do everything: change diapers, feed her, play with her, read to her and care for her – While he does nothing. An occasional diaper change or two and kisses and hugs periodically is not enough.

I am not taking this! If he's not going to help me with this baby, I'll put her in child care and let someone else raise her while I go and do what I want to do.

PART 3

WHAT DO I DO NOW?

LICENSED TO BUILD

Proverbs 24:27
> *Prepare thy work without, and make it fit for thyself*
> *in the field; and afterwards build thy house.*

Before a builder builds a home, she must have some knowledge about her field or vocation (building). She doesn't just send out the laborers and a beautiful home emerges from the earth. The builder understands that preparation is critical to a favorable or successful outcome. She should even be aware of the obstacles that may try to hinder her building process. She must be a good planner with calendar and schedule in hand. In other words, she has to get things ready and in line so that her efforts will net a home. In simple terms she must:

- Accept the plan drawn up by the architect
- Receive recommendations from those that she has given authority to in her life
- Get a building permit from the city

In the absence of preparation, there will not be any manifestation.

The Bible clearly illustrates this principle in the parable of the ten virgins. In the parable, there were 5 wise virgins and 5 foolish virgins. The five foolish virgins took their lamps to meet the bridegroom, but they didn't have any oil in them. The five wise virgins had their lamps and oil in hand in preparation to meet the bridegroom. While they waited for the bridegroom to come, all 10 slept. Later, when they got word that the bridegroom was on his way, the wise virgins trimmed their lamps in readiness to meet the bridegroom.

Meanwhile, the foolish ones didn't go and get any oil, instead they began to ask the wise ones for some of theirs. Not willing to give up their oil, the wise virgins told the foolish ones to go buy their own. While they went to buy, the bridegroom came for and married the wise ones. When the foolish virgins came back from getting oil, they asked the Lord to marry them as well and he disowned them. They must have been highly offended.

So what's the deal? Both groups started out with the same thing - lamps. However, the 5 virgins were wise because they actually prepared for their marriage. The first act of preparation was to get a lamp. The second was to have oil. The last, was to trim the lamp in readiness for the bridegroom. Once these things occurred, the marriage took place and now the virgins and the bridegroom were positioned to build a home.

The five foolish ones didn't prepare. They had lamps, but that wasn't enough. What good is a lamp without a trimmed wick and oil? Their willingness to get "right", after the fact, showed that they didn't take the marriage seriously.

Whether you are single or married, heed the wisdom of God in the parable and do the wise thing. You are the lamp. The oil represents the anointing. Get anointed and stay anointed. Set yourself apart. Be unwilling to compromise and live a life of obedience to the will of God, prayer and fasting.

Trim the lamp: Crucify the flesh. Allow the Holy Spirit to minister to you. Walk in the principles of the Word, so that you will experience the manifestation of his power in your marriage and household.

Preparation is critical to the success of our home building. If the preparation wasn't done prior to the marriage, don't delay - Get busy!! Remember: Where there's no preparation, there will be no manifestation. You can prepare by doing the following three things:

- Accept the plans of the Most High
- Esteem the Counsel of the Lord
- Get A Building Permit

Accept the plans of the Most High

Some of us have been through a lot. Some of us even feel as if no one really knows all that we have had to endure. Many of us walk around with our heads hanging down almost in allegiance to that old song that says, "Nobody knows the trouble I been through". We act as if not even God himself can fix our mess. Yet, that is far from the truth. God knows exactly what you have endured and what you may have even put yourself through.

He is the only architect in the universe that is qualified to teach us how to build. Having all knowledge, all wisdom and all understanding, He designed us with the utmost care and consideration. The Bible says that He fearfully and wonderfully made us.

He created the heavens and the earth. In Job 38 (Read it), God reminds Job that He laid the foundations of the earth, He determined the measures of the earth and stretched a measuring line on it. He fastened the foundations and laid the cornerstones. He marked the darkness with boundaries.

Just as He established the earth with laws of gravity, physics and the like, God has designed a plan for the way that a godly household is to be built, based upon his Word. He is so confident that you can get the job done, that he created the plan and established the principles for us to walk in way before the foundations of the earth were laid. His plan is illustrated here:

Jeremiah 29:11 (Amplified)
> *For I know the thoughts and plans that I have for you, says the Lord, thoughts and plans for welfare and peace and not for evil, to give you a hope in your final outcome.*

God wants us to have a successful marriage, a peaceful home

and an expectation for supernatural manifestation in our family life. Within the context of this book, your final outcome is to be a wise woman who establishes her household with godly principles and in divine excellence. In doing so, you will have a marriage and family life that the world can only dream about. Your home will neither fail nor fall apart, but will draw others to want to know Jesus in their own lives.

Esteem the Counsel of the Lord

Once we understand that God plans for us to have good success in our family life/marriage, we have to heed his information and instruction above anything else that we have heard or are comfortable with. No matter what our favorite Aunt told us, no matter what our dear parents taught us, no matter what our best friends told us - it should be unheeded - unless it was the counsel of the Lord.

The Word says that there are many ways or plans in a man's heart, but only the counsel of the Lord will stand. That means that no other counsel will produce the victorious, life-changing, permanent results that the Lord's counsel can.

So what is the counsel of the Lord? The counsel of the Lord is the solution to your situation from the Word of God. When someone gives you the counsel of the Lord, they don't give you their opinion or advice. They give you the Word. They give you biblical principles from the Word that will launch you toward success.

Sometimes the counsel of the Lord will come when the Holy Spirit ministers to you a specific plan of action based upon the Word and principles of God. Other times, the counsel of the Lord will come through a revelation of a biblical principle or scriptural reference. Any way it comes, godly counsel is always aligned with His word.

GET A BUILDING PERMIT

There are 3 simple steps that a woman must follow in order to be equipped to build:

- Be Born Again
- Filled with the Holy Spirit
- Committed to do the will of the Lord

First, you must be born again. You must believe and confess that Jesus is the son of God and then invite him into your heart to be your Lord and Savior.

Romans 10:9-10

> *That if thou shalt confess with thy mouth the Lord Jesus, and shalt believe in thine heart that God hath raised him from the dead, thou shalt be saved. For with the heart man believeth unto righteousness; and with the mouth confession is made unto salvation.*

Once you do this, God receives and acknowledges you as his daughter. As his daughter, you have the privilege of the Lord being in your life to help guide you as a shepherd does with sheep. But, a woman who hasn't submitted herself to God can't build a home according to God's specifications. She has no concept of godly principles and how they are supposed to work; therefore she can't get the blessed results that God has promised his daughters.

If you'd like to give your life to the Lord, there is no better time than now. At the back of this book there is a prayer that you can repeat and receive Jesus into your life as your Lord and Savior.

To maximize your relationship with the Lord, you need to get filled with the Spirit of God. It is the Holy Spirit that empowers you to build. Because in the building process, you will run into situations and instances where you will face the opposition of peers, family members, church members, or even your husband.

You need the power of God to help you resist the temptation to function like an unbeliever and to endure persecution from others who don't want to see you succeed. The Holy Spirit will provide that power. The Holy Spirit will minister direction, instruction, edification, exhortation, and comfort to you. Your obedience to His influence will help to keep you from stumbling and will cause others to see His divine participation in your life.

John 14:26

> *But the Comforter, which is the Holy Ghost, whom the Father will send in my name, he shall teach you*

*all things, and bring all things to your remem-
brance, whatsoever I have said unto you.*

Acts 1:8

> *But ye shall receive power, after that the Holy Ghost
> is come upon you: and ye shall be witnesses unto me
> both in Jerusalem, and in all Judaea, and in
> Samaria, and unto the uttermost part of the earth.*

If you would like to receive the power that God has designated for you to live a glorious and successful life, He is willing and ready to give it to you. Just spend some time thanking the Lord right now. You can worship Him right where you are. Tell Him how wonderful He is and has been to you. Thank Him for those things that You believe for Him to do in Your life and then pray the prayer located at the back of the book.. He is worthy!

Now make a commitment. Before you even begin learning about becoming the wise woman who builds, you must commit to use the biblical principles that she used, many of which are outlined later in this book. The Bible says that God hastens to perform his Word. That means if you are consistently applying biblical principles to your life, heeding wise counsel and confessing what the Word says about you, your marriage and family, then God will diligently and speedily manifest the promises associated with those principles.

Psalms 37:5

> *Commit thy way unto the LORD; trust also in him;
> and he shall bring it to pass.*

As you speak the following confession, expect for the Lord to minister direction to you. He has already set the direction in Jer. 29:11. Expect for him to manifest peace, prosperity, and blessings in your home. The Word says that our tongue is like the rudder of a ship. That means that with the words of our mouths, we can turn our situation in the direction that God desires for us to travel.

Commitment Confession

Father, your Word is a lamp to my feet and a light to my path. I commit to live my life in obedience to your Word. From this day forward, I commit to obey the principles that you have established for me to walk in. I will no longer look outside of your Word for the solution or answer to the situations in my life. You are the Most High God full of wisdom and glory. From this day forward, I will esteem your Word as the most excellent counsel and I will walk in it all of my days. I dedicate myself to replacing my will with Your will. As a result, I believe that you are giving me wisdom and insight for my family. My expectation is set and I know that you are doing marvelous things in my life and the life of my family, In Jesus name, Amen.

When you put this book down to do some chores, or go to bed, don't look at your current situation and let the enemy fool you into believing that things will never change. You are a daughter of the Most High God. You are filled with the very essence of God, the Holy Spirit. And now you have committed to use biblical principles to build a home that can only succeed.

OVERCOMING POTENTIAL FAITH ELIMINATORS

Internal Opposition - Conflicting Interests

Sometimes when a couple decides to end their marriage in what they believe to be an amiable manner, they site irreconcilable differences as their rational for the divorce. What they are really saying is that they have ideals, viewpoints, desires and future intentions that are in direct opposition to those of the other party.

Each of them is selfish and will not allow their desires to be second to the other. Both parties believe that since they can't get in agreement on the way that they ought to live, it would suit them better if they each did their own thing.

Believers experience an internal conflict as well. Unlike a couple who decided to live together in a marriage covenant, your flesh and the Holy Spirit don't get along from the moment you allow the Holy Spirit in your life. The desires of the flesh are to please self and the desires of the Holy Spirit are to please God. The flesh thinks that it knows best - but the Holy Spirit does know best. Therefore there is an ongoing conflict of interests between the two.

Galatians 5:17 (Amplified)

> *For the desires of the flesh are opposed to the [Holy] Spirit, and the [desires of] the Holy Spirit are opposed to the flesh (godless human nature); for these are antagonistic to each other [continually withstanding and in conflict with each other], so that you are not free but are prevented from doing what you desire to do.*

As you get into the next phase of this book, the Holy Spirit will continue to minister to you and give you biblical direction in building your home according to the Word of God. Some of what you will read and some of what God will tell you to do may go against what you are used to doing. Your flesh will want to rebel against the instruction and direction of the Holy Spirit because it doesn't want to be told the "right" way to do something.

Instead, the flesh wants a quick, temporary, self-pleasing, comfort zone type solution to the situation. So the flesh will try to get you to focus on negative aspects about yourself, your husband, or your children and not on what God said he would do in your home life.

Don't get distracted. Don't flirt with the ideas your flesh has to offer. God's winning alternative to following the flesh, is letting the Holy Spirit lead you. The Word shows us that when the flesh expresses its self-pleasing desires, the Holy Spirit will then confront those desires with the Word of God.

In other words, now that the Holy Spirit dwells in you, you can't do whatever your flesh wants you to do anymore, because the Holy Spirit will intervene and interject divine direction to you. Now you can either heed the Holy Spirit's direction and walk according to the ways of God, or heed the lusts of the flesh and be a disgrace in the eyes of God.

The Walk of Disgrace

Romans 8:8
> *So then they that are in the flesh cannot please God.*

The flesh is a sin-inclined, lust-driven, carnal part of our nature that must be crucified. It's not a cutesy little part of us that we expose from time to time so we can let our hair down. Neither is it convenient Christian slang to describe someone who is "acting up" or "naughty." There is nothing good about the flesh. The Bible tells us that a mind set on the flesh is hostile toward God and things that pertain to God.

The nature of the flesh is two-fold. First, it opposes the things of God. A primary example of two minds that were set on the flesh is the story of Adam and Eve. After the devil introduced a lie to them, they began to consider the lie so that their minds shifted from purposing or intending to obey God to imagining themselves as God.

Then, coaxed by their ungodly imaginations, their flesh began to desire what the devil told them, to the point that they chose to oppose God's plan for their lives and sinned. Not only did they touch the fruit, like God told them not to, they ate of the fruit, which was clearly an act of defiance toward God.

Second, the flesh is deceptive. When we allow the flesh to act out or make a decision, the result is illusive. Adam and Eve must have believed that they would really be like God if they partook of the fruit. However, they didn't get the outcome that they thought they would get. Instead, they were eternally evicted from the home that God created for them and they put themselves in the position to suffer and eventually die.

The Bible clearly defines about 17 different works (lusts) of the flesh:

Galatians 5:19-21
> *Now the works of the flesh are manifest, which are these; Adultery, fornication, uncleanness, lasciviousness, Idolatry, witchcraft, hatred, variance, emula-*

> *tions, wrath, strife, seditions, heresies; Envyings,*
> *murders, drunkenness, revellings, and such like of the*
> *which I tell you before, as I have also told you in time*
> *past, that they which do such things shall not inherit*
> *the kingdom of God.*

Some of you may be thinking that the fleshly works recorded in the passage of scripture don't apply to you. You may even be able to go down the list and cross off all of the things that you have never done. Maybe you never committed adultery or fornication. Maybe you never got drunk or committed murder. But those aren't the only fleshly acts listed. Not with the intent to condemn, but to simply get you to identify and better understand what the flesh looks like, I have listed some additional acts of the flesh that fall under some of the ones listed in Galatians 5. When you are led by your flesh, you may:

- Seek counsel from a psychic, fortune teller, numerologist or astrologist
- Do things to bring attention to yourself
- Rely upon old wives tales and superstitions as a way of life
- Become angry and staying angry (i.e.: people get on your bad side)
- Treat people differently depending upon what you hear or believe about them
- Decide to avoid some Believers just because you don't like them or their friends
- Look at others and conclude that they don't deserve what they have (job, car, husband)
- Hear gossip and believe it, without verifying it
- Side with a group or a person because you want the other group or person to suffer (get what they deserved)
- Judge someone's character and then try to get others to believe it (i.e.: so and so is probably fooling around with her boss ~ that's how she got that job)

Many of us don't purposefully evaluate whether we have been walking according to the desires of the flesh. All we know is that we have been doing what we want to do, whether it has worked or not, hoping that something would work or give in. But we ought to. The same way that the enemy came to Adam and Eve is the same way that he comes to us.

Illusive and hostile ideas introduced by the ultimate God-hater and unchecked by the Word of God, lure the flesh to act upon; will lead to death of a marriage or a family relationship. Walking in the flesh is detrimental to the success of a godly home. It is impossible to build and complete a building in the flesh.

The Flesh Brings Destruction

Galatians 6:8a

> *For he that soweth to his flesh shall of the flesh reap corruption.*

In the word, God has identified some situations where people have allowed their flesh to be in control. They have chosen not to listen to the Lord, but instead they fine tuned their ears to listen to and then act upon their own desires. As a result, their self-perceived good intentions were ultimately self-destructive.

Tower of Babel
Genesis 11:1-9

> *[1] And the whole earth was of one language, and of one speech.*
> *[2] And it came to pass, as they journeyed from the east, that they found a plain in land of Shinar, and they dwelt there.*
> *[3] And they said one to another, Go to, let us make brick, and burn them thoroughly. And they had brick for stone and slime had they for mortar.*
> *[4] And they said, Go to, let us build a city and a tower, whose top may reach unto heaven; and let us make*

us a name, lest we be scattered abroad upon the face of the whole earth.
5And the Lord came down to see the city and the tower, which the children of men builded.
6And the Lord said, Behold, the people is one, and they have all one language; and this they begin to do: and now nothing will be restrained from them, which they have imagined to do.
7Go to, let us go down, and there confound their language, that they may not understand one another's speech.
8So the Lord scattered them abroad from thence upon the face of all the earth: and they left off to build the city.
9Therefore is the name of it called Babel; because the Lord did there confound the language of all the earth and from thence did the Lord scatter them abroad upon the face of all the earth.

This biblical example illustrates the method in which the people allowed their fleshly desires to pervert Godly principles, resulting in their ultimate failure and confusion. Remember, the nature of the flesh is to oppose the things of God. There is nothing good in it.

Godly Principle 1 - Agreement

Agreement is powerful. The Word tells us that two people can't even unite unless they agree. It also tells us that wherever two or more are gathered in his name, that He will be in the midst of them. When we agree to submit ourselves to the Lord's way of doing things, we invite the presence of God in our midst.

Flesh Failure 1

The whole earth came together in flesh-based agreement. They were driven by their lusts to glorify themselves and to impress God. It was a dangerous move that cost them their understanding. The scriptures say that God confounded their language. Therefore, they could no longer be understood by each other anymore.

Practical Insight

When a husband and a wife agree amiss (not in line with the Word or the Spirit of God, but with the desires of the flesh), they invite confusion into their midst. In essence, they set themselves to believe for a thing without godly insight or direction and eventually they become confused because what they agreed upon doesn't manifest for them.

Godly Principle 2 - Submission

Submission is God's protective order. When we submit ourselves unto God, and resist the devil, then he will flee. Submission is an act of humbling oneself to the plan of God and opposing all other plans that interfere with it.

Flesh Failure 2

The people of the earth set up their own protective measure. They figured that if they made a name for themselves, that they wouldn't be scattered abroad. So, instead of humbling themselves and submitting their plan to God for his consent, they believed that they could impress Him with their plan. God ended their building project.

Practical Insight

When a husband and a wife fail to submit themselves and their plans to the Lord, yet they continue in their own experience-based wisdom, they become building-impaired. Their ability to establish a household that reflects the glory of the Lord is blocked. Confused and disillusioned by the numerous failures and the near successes, they eventually give up building and their households become fragmented.

Walking In The Spirit

Galatians 5:16

> *But I say walk and live [habitually] in the [Holy] Spirit [responsive to and controlled and guided by the Spirit]; then you will certainly not gratify the*

cravings and desires of the flesh (of human nature without God).

For many of us, walking is almost automatic. We don't have to contemplate whether or not we are going to walk when we want to go to the kitchen for a snack. We don't have to contemplate whether or not we need to walk in order to get from the car to the shopping mall. If we are going to get a snack or go buy some clothes, we know that we will have to walk to get them. So with these goals in mind, we simply stand up and start moving our legs in the desired direction.

Walking in the Spirit should be automatic in the life of every Believer. You need the presence of the Lord in your home, marriage, family. You need wisdom on how to manage your home, meet the needs of your children and your husband. You need to know how to obtain and maintain peace while handling home, career and even ministry.

God has promised you a successful and blessed marriage, wisdom in every area of your life, abundant peace, prosperity in finances and health, and favor among men, just to name a few. With these promises in mind, we must stand (uncompromisingly) in the word of God and stand in faith (believing and not doubting his word), so that we can begin to move in the direction that the Lord has planned for us.

The Spirit of God is the core or essence of who he is. When we operate in the word, with faith, and walk under the guidance of the Holy Spirit, we are experiencing direction from the core of God's thoughts, plans, and teaching for our lives.

Here is an acrostic that I call C.O.R.E. This may help you to remember that you need to exercise your faith and the word by sowing the following faith-filled/word-based actions:

- Confess what the Word says about you, your marriage and your family
- God released his word to create something from nothing. Confessing God's word over your life, will create in you the ability to see yourself like he sees you and then

to become that way.
- Obey the biblical principles illustrated in the word
- The foundations of the earth were framed by principles designed by God. Everything living and nonliving must obey Him.
- Reject ungodly counsel, non-biblical advice, and carnal m.o.'s
- God ejected Lucifer from heaven for rebelliousness. We too must reject those things that don't line up with and rebel against the Word.
- Expect God to manifest his presence in your life
- God sent forth his Word to accomplish the tasks he had for it to accomplish, it will never return void.

Walking in the Spirit is a daily walk. If you use your faith and the word of God to exercise C.O.R.E. periodically or when a crisis arises, you will be on a spiritual seesaw. Sometimes you will believe God; sometimes you will listen to unwise counsel. Sometimes you will get results, sometimes you won't.

However, by using your faith and the word of God daily and exercising C.O.R.E. regularly, you can expect to be permanently changed. We can expect a level of growth and spiritual maturity that is unable to be accomplished without his power.

The Bible lists several characteristics that will develop as a result of walking in the Spirit. Galatians 5 calls these characteristics the fruit of the Spirit: love, joy, peace, patience, kindness, goodness, faithfulness, gentleness, and self-control. This is the fruit that you must bear in order to help you endure while your circumstances are changing.

C.O.R.E. Walkers
Confession ~ Obedience ~ Rejection of carnal methods ~ Expectation of Godly Manifestation

Abraham & Sarah

Confession

When God changed Abram's name to Abraham, he changed Sarai's name to Sarah. When he called him father of many nations, he called her mother of many nations. Each time she said his name, she confessed God's purpose over his life. Each time he said her name, he confessed God's purpose over her life. So that even though her age and her barrenness was thought to be a natural impediment to bringing forth the promised son, Isaac - They spoke in line with God's Word and the word manifested the change.

Obedience

God's covenant with Abraham was conditional. In order for it to come to pass, Abraham had to agree to live a life of obedience and faith towards God. When the Lord told him to get out of his country, which was a familiar and comfortable place, and follow his direction (no matter how distant or unfamiliar) he chose to obey.

Rejection of carnal methods

After Abraham left Egypt, with his wife and Lot, and settled with their belongings, the Bible says that there was strife between his men and Lot's men. So when they went their separate ways, Abraham chose to dwell in Canaan and Lot chose to dwell in cities that were close to the sinful and wicked city of Sodom. Abraham was determined to go in the opposite direction that Lot was going in.

Abraham said that if Lot wanted to go left, then he would go right and vice versa. Abraham could've chosen the well watered plain where Lot went, but Abraham had a mind to obey and follow God. Therefore, he chose not to live where wickedness and carnality thrived.

Expectation of God's Manifestation

Living a life of barrenness for nearly a century caused them to have no expectation or hope for children. But, after Abraham and Sarah clearly heard from God, they had hope. That hope became the substance from which their faith could grow. Now, they could exercise their faith in expectation to receive the son that God promised to them.

External Opposition

2 Corinthians 2:11
Lest Satan should get an advantage of us: for we are not ignorant of his devices.

Now that we've exposed the internal opposition – the flesh, there is another type of opposition that the woman of God will face – an external one. The enemy will attempt to hinder your spirit led building process or completely stop you from doing things God's way. It's not a personal thing. The devil really wants to get at God; but he wants to use God's most precious creation to do it. Ultimately, the enemy will try to persuade us to forsake the plan of God for our households. Therefore, we must know how he will attack. We must know how he creeps into the relationship that we have with our spouses and children.

There are several ways that the devil can coax you into dismissing the plan of God for your life. One method that he uses is distraction. He attempts to get you to believe that the others around you - who haven't fully committed to do the will of God, are doing alright. These people are in a stagnant state of mediocrity. God hasn't called us to just exist in him, or be average. He called our families to be a glorious example of his manifestation in the earth.

Yet, even with this insight, he'll continue to show you irrelevant and false examples of people who appear to have a blessed family life, yet they aren't progressing from glory to glory. In all of these efforts, his hope is that you will do nothing to bring your home life to a level of blessing and glory that God has ordained for you.

The enemy will also come by way of an unbeliever. An unbeliever is someone who has a perverted belief system. This person can be one who isn't a Christian, or it could also be a Christian who has chosen not to believe God in the area of building and restoring the household to exemplify the glory and power of God.

Instead of using their ability to believe God, the unbeliever has chosen to put his trust in man, the world, and their ways. What they are actually doing is doubting the fact that God and His way is the only solution to living an abundantly blessed and successful life. The unbeliever spews doubt and distrust in the success that biblical homebuilding will bring, but focuses on the current, dissatisfying, status of the home.

Your enemy is the devil who desires to see your demise, downfall, and utter destruction. People are not your enemies. However, if a person is not being led of the Lord and God is not their Father, they are prime property for the devil to use. These people make it a practice to do and say things with the intent to hurt or destroy you. Anyone who is not submitted to the Lord is fair game for the devil to use: co-workers, family members, even some brothers or sisters in the Lord. As Believers, we are supposed to pray for them.

So how do we overcome and forge ahead when the devil is opposing our godly success so hard? How do we handle those who hate our commitment to do things according to the Word? Our example is found in the book of Nehemiah. Nehemiah was a servant of the Lord who had to overcome demonic opposition from his enemies in order for him to successfully build Jerusalem's wall with the anointing of the Lord.

Victory Testimony
When my husband and I were in the stages of beginning to build our home biblically, we encountered, endured, and successfully defeated both internal and external opposition. Internally, my flesh was screaming all types of ungodly things to me. It told me to do as I pleased and don't worry about him. It told me that I was on my own and that he wasn't there for me. It even told me that he wasn't as spiritually mature as I was in some areas - like he was slow to hear from God. Yet all along, the spirit of God ministered the truth

of his word and the truth of the situation. I had to listen and do what the Lord said in order to win.

Then I had to defeat the enemy externally. There were unbelieving "Christians" that said that our marriage wouldn't work. There were family members who didn't want to see us work it out and when they found out that we were going to do all that we could biblically to have the marriage God was pleased with, they neglected to talk to us for years. Not one year, but years, plural. These are just a few of the things that I went through. But, God ministered to me in the first year of my marriage from the book of Nehemiah and I gleaned all that I could from it to help me successfully defeat the enemy's opposition to the plan of success and abundance that God had for my marriage and family life.

In the following pages, we will look at the opposition that Nehemiah faced, his response to that opposition, and the wise counsel that we can act upon in our own lives. I followed the wisdom that I received from this example and I won!!!

Look at what happened (in summary) to Nehemiah when He had the task of building:

Nehemiah got word that Jerusalem's walls were broken down, the gates were burned, and the people were in serious trouble and disgrace. Moved with compassion, Nehemiah wept, mourned, and fasted and prayed to God about the situation.

In his prayer, Nehemiah asked forgiveness for disobeying the laws, decrees and commands (the Word) that he gave to Moses. He reminded God that he promised to restore and redeem those who went astray, if they in turn would submit and obey God's commandments. Then he asked the Lord to honor this promise for him and all of those who would do so and to give him favor as he went forth to build.

The Bible says that the hand of the Lord was on Nehemiah as he rebuilt the wall. However, when his enemies and other unbelievers heard the news, they began to actively and unsuccessfully come against the plan of God. Each time Nehemiah faced opposition and persecution from these evil forces, his response strengthened his faith and he was able to defeat the enemy's wicked scheme.

Nehemiah experienced persecution at least 7 times as he went forth under the anointing to build. However, he overcame the opposition and went forth victoriously and successfully completed the building project. As we go forth to build, there are some things that we can learn from Nehemiah's success. You may not know how the enemy plans to oppose you beforehand, however if you respond with the wisdom of God, so that you will not lose your anointing to build.

Nehemiah Overcomes Opposition

Opposition #1 (Nehemiah 2:10)

When Nehemiah's enemies, Sanballat and Tobiah heard that he cared about the destruction in Jerusalem, they were very troubled.

Wise Response

Having already prayed and standing in faith that God would restore the destruction; Nehemiah surveyed the damage and only told those who would support him that he intended to rebuild the wall. Those whom he told were in agreement and the Bible says that they strengthened their hands to build.

Wise Counsel

After you have decided to believe and then prayed that God would build or rebuild your home, tell only those who will be in faith with you or will support you in your godly efforts. Only those who believe that God will do this in your life are willing to help you and lift you up in prayer.

Opposition #2 (Nehemiah 2:19)

Once Sanballat and Tobiah found out what Nehemiah intended to do, they ridiculed and hated him for it. Then they mocked him and suggested that in building the wall, he was rebelling against the king. (It sounds like they're getting ready to start spreading lies, doesn't it?)

Wise Response

Keeping focus on the promise that God made to Nehemiah and the goal (to rebuild), he told his enemies that God would prosper them in their endeavor and that they had no authority to stop it otherwise. Each time Nehemiah (and those who helped) built a gate of the city, they sanctified it.

Wise Counsel

Focus on the promise that God has for you as you build or rebuild according to God's specifications. When your unbelieving co-workers, relatives, church folks or enemies begin to spew unbelief or begin to mock your efforts, keep standing on the Word. They have no authority to stop it. You, like Nehemiah, have the hand of the Lord upon you when you commit to build according to his Word.

Opposition #3 (Nehemiah 4:1-3)

Sanballat heard that the wall was being built and in an angry rage, he ridiculed them. He called them feeble, made fun of what they were doing, and slandered God in the process. Tobiah discounted their endeavors so much that he told them that whatever they tried to build would be so weak it would collapse under pressure.

Wise Response

Having heard about his enemy's and the unbeliever's response, Nehemiah prayed and asked the Lord to deal with them according to their evilness.

Wise Counsel

When and if you hear any lies, slander, or words of disbelief in God's plan for your household don't get in the flesh. Stay in the Spirit and ask the Lord to deal with them. Let him handle the situation. Vengeance doesn't belong to us.

Opposition #4 (Nehemiah 4:7-8)

When Sanballat and Tobiah, etc. heard that the wall was almost finished, they became very angry again. So, they plotted to fight Nehemiah in order to disturb and hinder the building process.

Wise Response
Nehemiah prayed to the Lord and watched for any potential attacks.

Wise Counsel
When those enemies or unbelievers around you still look at you crazy and with disgust or ridicule, continue to pray for them. Next, be ready to resist the enemy's suggestions to follow flesh or the world's way of doing things. Don't think about what you are going to do after you are in the situation. Have a plan established beforehand. Be ready to resist the enemy. But here is the key: We must submit our way to God, resist the devil, and then he will flee. He won't go anywhere until we submit and do things God's way.

Opposition #5 (Nehemiah 4:11)

Nehemiah's adversaries plotted to kill them because of their dedication and commitment to follow through with the plan to build.

Wise Response
He put armed men behind the weak areas of the wall. The weak areas were areas that weren't completely fortified yet. They needed to be guarded because they weren't quite strong enough to withstand physical attack. He also told fear to go.

Wise Counsel
The devil will try to go for the jugular vein at some point. He will try to push your hot button and strategically set up a road block to where you will have to use supernatural strength not to slip back

into your old carnal way of handling things. Ask some of those who
are fortified in faith, to hold you up in prayer in this area of weakness. Continue to stand in faith, on the Word, and don't allow the
fear of things not changing lure you into following fleshly desires.

Opposition #6 (Nehemiah 6:1-7)

When the enemies found that the wall was just about finished,
they lied and told him that they heard that he was about to make the
announcement that he would be king of Judah, so they wanted to
meet with him. This was their plot to harm him.

Wise Response
He told his enemies that he did not plan to proclaim himself as
king and that they were making all of that up in their heads. He
recognized that they were trying to get him to be afraid of finishing
the building project and he asked the Lord to strengthen his hands.

Wise Counsel
The enemy will try to slander you, lie on you, and get you to
focus on stuff that isn't biblically true about your household. You
must stay focused and in faith, not in fear, and ask the Lord to
strengthen you. He will complete the good work you started in faith.

Opposition #7 (Nehemiah 6:12)

The enemies hired an invalid to give false prophecy to
Nehemiah with the hope that he would believe the lie, get in fear
and lose faith in what God promised to do.

Wise Response
Fully aware that the prophecy was false, Nehemiah recognized
that the enemies tried to frame him. He prayed to God concerning
their wickedness again, and then finished the wall.

Wise Counsel

As you stay focused on what God promised you in his Word, you will be able to detect and defeat the enemy no matter how he comes.

The key to Nehemiah's successful defeat of the demonic opposition was that he stayed focused on the promises of God. He held on to the fact that God said that if they repented and began to walk in the ways of the Lord, he would restore them. So no matter how cunning, wicked or evil the enemy tried to be, he didn't allow any obstacle to stand in his way. He dismissed fear, he fortified himself with believers, and he told the enemy that he had no authority in this matter.

The word says that God prevented their evil and wicked plans from being effective. Each time he accomplished the building of a wall gate, he sanctified it. In the end, when the enemies found out that the wall was complete, they were afraid and they felt stupid, because they knew that only God could have done such a thing.

As it was with Nehemiah, so it is with us. If you will hold onto the promise of God restoring, rebuilding, or building your household and not allow the tricks of the enemy to hinder you, nothing will stand in your way. You will succeed! You will win!! The enemy has no authority in this matter if you follow the biblical house-building principles from the Word.

Ask those who are in faith with you to keep your household in prayer, tell fear to go, walk in the Spirit of the Lord and watch the Lord establish your home. In the end, your enemies and the unbelievers will feel stupid and they will know that the hand of the Lord was upon you and anointed you to build.

After I obtained victory in defeating the enemy's opposition to my house building efforts, those relatives that didn't talk to me for years, began to talk to me. Those who said it couldn't be done called to apologize for the things that they said and thought in secret.

RECYCLABLE TOOLS
You use the same tools to build as you do to tear down -

Just about everyone is familiar with the old game show "Let's Make A Deal". In order to become a contestant, the audience member had to have one of the eccentric or sometimes very common items that the host requested. With this as the qualifier, the contestant could make a deal to trade the item for a small prize or some money. If the player came out ahead, they advanced to dealing for an even larger prize behind one of three doors. Only one of the doors had the most desirable prize behind it.

Although God doesn't play a game of chance with us, there are some components of this game that remind me of how God deals with us. His desire and plan for us, according to Jer. 29:11, is to prosper in every way and to give us a hope and future.

God's execution of this plan is simple. His desire is that we will forsake foolishness and obtain his wisdom. Through his Word and by his Spirit, he will give us insight into how to live an abundantly blessed life. Then he lets us choose whether or not we want to trade our current way of doing things for his blessed way of doing things. Once we make a decision to go for what he wants us to go for, we begin to see his manifestation in our lives.

But, like the game show, the next level is even more exciting. We can either keep the lifestyle that we've chosen where we see God beginning to move in our homes and families or we can choose something even greater. Now we must decide whether we want to keep our current situation or go for an even greater and more consistent manifestation of God's power in our lives.

At this level, we are fully aware of the trade offs to be made. We must choose to let him establish our households, starting with us – or we can keep the average Christian lifestyle that seems to be comfortable at this point. The choice is ours to make.

Door number one holds the reward of establishing our homes our way, according to the flesh – leading to a lifestyle of disappointments, frustration, and death. Door number 2 holds the reward of establishing our homes the world's way, according to the foolishness that the world esteems as wisdom – leading to a lifestyle of consistent set backs and a life filled with trials and errors. Door number 3 holds the reward of establishing our homes God's way, according to his specifications – leading to a lifestyle of peace, joy, abundance, and victory. Every woman must make this choice.

PART 4

ENOUGH IS ENOUGH

WISE WOMEN FORSAKE WORLDLY WISDOM

Proverbs 4:7
> *Wisdom is the principal thing; therefore get wisdom:*
> *and with all thy getting get understanding.*

Proverbs 9:10
> *The fear of the LORD is the beginning of wisdom,*
> *and the knowledge of the Holy One is understanding.*

So how do you become wise? How do you just cast worldly wisdom aside when you've relied on it for such a long time? Well, it starts with the act of fearing the Lord. This one quality caused the woman in Prov. 31 to be honored and praised by her husband, children and those she came in contact with. She received the distinction of being an excellent wife because of the wisdom she obtained, but it all started with the fear of the Lord.

Prov. 31:30
> *Favour is deceitful, and beauty is vain: but a woman*
> *that feareth the LORD, she shall be praised.*

Although many people have tried to complicate the principle of fearing God, it is quite simple. Fearing the Lord is summed up here:

Proverbs 8:13
> *The fear of the LORD is to hate evil: pride, and arrogancy, and the evil way, and the froward mouth, do I hate.*

When a person hates something, they oppose it. They don't make excuses for it and they don't rationalize its existence. As Believers, we are supposed to combat the thing that we hate with the Word of God, so that thing doesn't defile our hearts. In the context of this scripture, wisdom opposes:

- Evil – wickedness, mischief, adversity, distress
- Pride and arrogancy – personal exaltation
- Evil way – wicked, destructive habits; hurtful way of life
- Froward mouth – perverse mouth; speaking those things that are not in line with the Word of God

As a result of fearing the Lord, God has promised us some great things. There are probably many more, but here are a few:

Promises of Fearing the Lord

- Good Understanding

Psalms 111:10
> *The fear of the LORD is the beginning of wisdom: a good understanding have all they that do his commandments: his praise endureth for ever.*

- Knowledge

Proverbs 1:7
> *The fear of the LORD is the beginning of knowledge: but fools despise wisdom and instruction.*

- Long Life

Proverbs 10:27
The fear of the LORD prolongeth days: but the years of the wicked shall be shortened.

- Strong Confidence & Refuge for Your Children

Proverbs 14:26
In the fear of the LORD is strong confidence: and his children shall have a place of refuge.

- Fountain of Life

Proverbs 14:27
The fear of the LORD is a fountain of life, to depart from the snares of death.

- Riches, Honor and Life

Proverbs 22:4
By humility and the fear of the LORD are riches, and honour, and life.

When a woman of God decides to abandon the world's way of doing things in exchange for God's way of doing things, wisdom emerges. As I shed the world's way of doing things and focused on fearing the Lord, wisdom began to flow from me as never before. In the next several pages, I will share the wisdom that God gave me as I rejected the 7 carnal beliefs that had the potential to wreck my household.

TRUST HIM

Psalm 118:8, 9
>*It is better to trust in the Lord than to put confidence in man.*
>*It is better to trust in the Lord than to put confidence in princes.*

Proverbs 29:25
>*The fear of man bringeth a snare: but whoso putteth his trust in the Lord shall be safe.*

The world is double-minded. On one hand, they say you can't trust men, not even your husband. On the other hand they say that trust is the key ingredient to a successful marriage. Many women have these opposing views because their worldly beliefs have backfired on them. They actually put their trust in men and as a result they got hurt. Yet they still yearn for a potential mate or husband to put their trust in. And since neither one of these views is the counsel of the Lord - neither one is true.

When my husband and I first married, I told him something that he said was profound - yet at first offensive. I told him that I didn't trust him. Did I tell him that because:

a. I thought he was sneaky, conniving or deceitful
b. I thought he would harm me and our future children
c. I believed he would desert me, abuse me or commit adultery
d. I was retaliating in the midst of a heated argument with the intentions of hurting him

The answer is: none of the above

As a wife, as a woman of God, I knew my husband's character. I knew that I could trust him. He was and still is a man of great integrity. What I meant by that statement was that I didn't and wouldn't put my trust in him. My telling him this was based upon a Word God spoke to me when he healed me from the past hurts: Put not your trust in princes, nor in the son of man, in whom there is no help - Psalm 146:3.

When a wife puts her trust in her husband, she begins to focus on what he is able to do out of his own strength, talents, skills and capabilities. In essence, leaving little room for what the Lord can and will do through him. Her focus becomes husband centered and not God centered. When this happens, she eventually becomes disappointed and let down when he can't meet the expectations that she has set for him and the family.

A wise woman can learn to trust her husband, but she puts her trust in the Lord. Though he may bring smiles to my face and laughter to my heart, I don't rely upon my husband to make me happy. Neither do I allow his weaknesses make me sad or depressed - my trust is in the Lord. He protects me. If my husband, who is the head of our household, makes a decision that goes against what I believe to be the right thing to do, the Bible says that if I put my trust in the Lord then I will be safe; He will be a shield to me.

Putting my trust in the Lord is a state of being. I put it there and it stays there. I rest in it. I have full knowledge that it exists and the Lord God will never fall short. He will always meet above and beyond any expectation that I have in any situation. My Father will never let me down.

WHAT HE REALLY WANTS IS . . . . . .

Proverbs 31:10 (Amplified)
> *A capable, intelligent, and virtuous woman - who is he who can find her? She is far more precious than jewels and her value is far above rubies or pearls.*

I lacked understanding when I thought that my husband wanted to be locked up in the bedroom for 24 hours a day. I believed this lie as if it was the truth. He had waited 29 years to be married, and now he just wanted to physically love me. I thought that he didn't care much about what I wanted and who I could become, he just wanted sex. Then the Lord began to impart his wisdom to me on the situation. He showed me that my husband and every other husband wanted a virtuous woman for a wife.

As adolescent boys, enter adulthood, they often share some-thing in common. Many of them want a girlfriend who is an atten-tion-getter. Some may not want to admit it, but they want the honor roll student, honest, unwavering, caring, benevolent, understanding, athletic, enthusiastic, well-groomed, outgoing, potential wife-type girl. The type of girl that is unapproachable in their eyes, because some would say that she is too good for them. They want the kind of girl that would enhance their overall well-being.

Well when you look at Prov. 31 (verses 10-31), we see a woman, empowered by the Spirit of God, who had a radiant lifestyle worthy of others attention. This woman had integrity, she was peaceable, not meddling in the affairs of others, considerate, benevolent, wise, loving, gentle, kind, creative, strong, and bold, just to name a few. She was an excellent wife and her husband had favor in the land. She didn't bring him shame, only blessing. She feared the Lord.

God showed me that he placed within every man, a deep-seated desire for a woman who is "all of that" and more. In the natural many boys are exposed to girls who have some of the seed characteristics of the virtuous woman. However, to the man whose mother never taught him what to look for in a wife, this desire becomes an illusion - some-thing that he sees in principle yet is never naturally manifested.

Think of it this way, what if God planted in man the desire for a virtuous wife, yet his mother never watered it with God's descrip-tion (expectation) for this woman? Or what if the majority of girls that he was exposed to never learned how to obtain the characteris-tics of a virtuous woman?

Would the guy look for this godly proto-type? Probably not. He would actually choose the easy way out and look for the female play mate, unless he had God-fearing women who taught him what a virtuous woman looked like according to the Word.

Does this change the fact that he wants a virtuous woman? Not hardly. He wants a wife committed to excellence in every area of her life: in her ministry to her husband and children, in business, in personal friendships/relationships, and her personal relationship with God.

I needed to become the virtuous woman God desired for me to be. Once God revealed this to me, I made some changes. I made a commitment to find out what God wanted me to do, so that I could become who he wanted me to become. I learned that I had to:

- Seek the Lord and His counsel
- Work at becoming an excellent wife
- Desire what the Lord had for me
- Not give up
- Seek and Learn more effective ways to minister to my family
- Get up, even if I fell, until I overcame my weaknesses with the Word
- Let go of my temper, change my confession, and obtain a new attitude
- Cease murmuring and complaining and idol chatter
- Forsake those things that were detrimental to my spiritual growth
- Exercise obedience to God and his ways, including my husband

I'M IN CONTROL

Proverbs 31:26

> *She openeth her mouth with wisdom; and in her tongue is the law of kindness.*

Ecclesiastes 10:12

> *The words of a wise man's mouth are gracious; but the lips of a fool will swallow up himself.*

Proverbs 8:8 (Amplified)

> *All of the words of my mouth are righteous (upright and in right standing with God); there is nothing contrary to truth or crooked in them.*

As you read through the lies that the foolish woman believed, you saw how they influenced the young girl's perception of men from youth through adulthood and then marriage. Her former experiences with men coupled with her exposure to other's experiences with them helped to shape her opinion of them.

When she looked at her husband, she saw him as the epitome of male stereo-types: controlling, sex fiends, lacking emotions, demanding, unhelpful, and stupid. In turn, she began to receive and accept these views into her heart. Then, she began calling him (in her mind, behind his back, and sometimes in his face): stupid, untrustworthy, controlling, uncaring, etc. Instead of communicating her displeasure in his attitude or behavior in a mature fashion, she resorted to calling him names and laughing at dumb male jokes.

Her heart was so full of negative things about men, that eventually she became hostile toward him. When he came home from work, she would despise his presence and they would almost immediately argue.

Luke 6:45

> *A good man out of the good treasure of his heart*
> *bringeth forth that which is good; and an evil man*
> *out of the evil treasure of his heart bringeth forth*
> *what is evil: for of the abundance of the heart his*
> *mouth speaketh.*

God has created our hearts with the capacity to hold things dear to us like treasure. At the same time, He has created us with the ability to choose what we treasure: good or evil. The process that our minds and hearts go through when we begin to hold something dear to us stays the same no matter what we treasure.

For instance, when you treasure something good, you hold on to it and every memory associated with it. You don't allow anything to come between it and yourself. Nothing can change or distort the picture you have conjured up in your mind about it.

Every time you think upon it, wonderful feelings, sweet aromas, and happy moments come to mind. It's like when some people say they fall in love. They remember the day, time, place, what they wore, what he wore, the music, what the people around them looked like, etc...

When you treasure something bad, you hold on to it and every memory associated with it as well. You don't allow anything to come between that experience and how you view it. Every time you think about it, you feel betrayed, irritated, discouraged, furious, and maybe even vindictive. Bitterness and unforgiveness are the choice feelings when you choose to hold on to bad treasures. Some people say that this is how they felt when their husbands ditched them for another woman. They remembered the day they found out, the time, what was said and how he said it.

The point here is that we can either choose to fill our hearts with honorable, pure, just thoughts (Philippians 4:8) or we can choose to fill them with bad memories, vile thoughts, beliefs and opinions. IT IS YOUR CHOICE. The Lord instructs us in Proverbs 4:23 to guard our hearts with all diligence.

That means that we are supposed to judge whether the ideas, thoughts, opinions or beliefs that we have heard line up with what the Word of God says before we receive them into our hearts. Because once we believe something in our hearts, it becomes truth to us - even if it is a lie. And eventually, our mouths will reveal our beliefs ~ godly or ungodly, truth or a lie.

We have heard them tell jokes about the inadequacies of husbands, the lacking characteristics of males, the foolishness of marriage, and they mock the headship role of the husband likening it to a dictatorship. The devil desperately wants to steal, kill and destroy marriages.

First, he desires to steal the headship role from the husband, by deceiving some wives into thinking that they need to be in control all of the time. Then he distorts and perverts that idea to: he's trying to control me. Being controlling is not the same as being the God-ordained head in a marriage. One dictionary defines control as the ability or authority to manage or direct.

Many women have had negative incidents or situations in which a male employer has misused his authority as a manager or supervisor and stepped over into the realm of verbal abuse, discrimination, or even sexual harassment. Some wives have experienced husbands who, ignorant of their godly responsibility as head of their households, have taken this assignment and turned it into a manipulative role.

Without a doubt, misuse of authority is abuse. However, the devil knows that if he can expose us to enough authority abusing and controlling men, either in real life or on television, then he can eventually persuade us to see some similar characteristics in our husbands, ultimately viewing them as controlling.

Second, he desires to destroy the marriage by persuading us that we ought to assume the headship role. This is the trap that I fell into. I listened to the enemy long enough for him to convince me that my intelligence had been insulted just by the mere fact that my husband was the head of our household - even though God is the one who created this position before my husband even existed. Then he told me that I didn't have to be treated like a second class citizen, I had a mind of my own, and therefore I needed to be in control.

As a result, I became desensitized to my husband's true character and begin to act as if he didn't deserve the authority that God had given him and he needed a replacement - me. Eventually my mouth birthed strife into our marriage as I regurgitated what I'd been digesting.

Last, he hopes that the burdens or responsibilities that come with the role of headship - will kill us (wives) because we are not designed to carry this type of responsibility in a marriage relationship. He wants us to get stressed out, overwhelmed, and physically or mentally sick over burdens that he didn't entitle us to carry: I call them unauthorized burdens, and I had plenty of them.

In the midst of my situation the wisdom of the Lord spoke to me. He brought me to the scripture that said Jesus' yoke is easy and his burden is light. We are authorized to carry and then cast only the burdens that he intended for us. Those burdens assigned to our husbands are so heavy for us, that we have serious problems casting them over to the Lord. They can cast them much more easily without worry, stress or strain.

The desire that I had to control my marriage was not of God, but the task of controlling my mouth was. Now this assignment has truly been ordained by God. The Bible says in Proverbs 15:28 that the heart of the righteous studies to answer, but the mouth of the wicked pours out evil things.

We have been given the duty, if we want to be wise, to control or manage the words of our mouths. If we will take the Word of God, let it replace our opinions, and truly believe what it says then we won't receive the junk that the world (via the devil) puts before us and our hearts will be full of good things.

I AM A PRINCESS

The world views marriage and family apart from the wisdom of God. To many of them, marriage is a fantasy-like state where 2 people, with 2 different careers live a life full of compromise in order to please one another; and children are an accessory. The foolishness of their wisdom has infiltrated the minds of many women and influenced them to believe that in order to be successful in life; they must be willing to make a sacrifice. The sacrifice requires the temporary abandonment and neglect of their marriage and family relationships. As a result, husbands and wives, parents and their children no longer grow together, they fall apart.

As a young pre-married woman, I began to learn about the importance of unity and agreement in a marriage, but my mind wasn't renewed yet. Consequently, I functioned with a carnal mind-set and much worldly wisdom my first year of marriage, which caused a myriad of problems.

My first conflict became the struggle between God's plan for me as a married woman and my plan for my life as a married woman. The ideas, thoughts, desires and plans that I had for myself and my career before I married may have been acceptable for me as a single person. Before, I knew what God had for me to do and I had even discussed it with my fiancé before we married. Yet, once I married I had to reconsider and pray for God's new plan because now it involved another person, my husband.

My Plan
I felt like I had a very well thought out strategy. I wanted to have children while I was young and energetic, I wanted to further

my education, and I didn't want any daycare raising our children. So, I intended to work from home. I figured that I would become pregnant and start graduate school. Then, with my extra schooling, I would establish myself as a Christian screenplay writer, while free-lancing from home and keeping our baby with me. All of these goals were attainable, given the level of energy, determination, and faith to succeed that I had. So I shared them with my husband with the hope that he would agree and encourage me to go for it.

Although he agreed with me overall, he didn't want to have children right away. He wanted to wait a few years to have children so he could spend time with me alone. He thought that we needed time to come together as one, since we had just come from a 2 _ year long-distance engagement. Prior to this point, neither one of us submitted our desires to the Lord to find out what He really wanted us to do.

Well, not long after this intense discussion, I became pregnant. I was extremely excited. I had one down and one more to go. I just knew that it wouldn't be long before I would enroll in a graduate program at a university nearby. But one day when I began to talk to my husband about going to school again, he told me that he would pray about it and that I should pray about it again. He had a very good salary, but we had a small amount of debt to eliminate, he needed my support at home, and I was due around the time I needed to enroll.

His suggestion for me to go and pray about it again made me mad. I figured that I didn't need to pray about it. I already knew that I wanted to go to school and that was that! Grudgingly, I prayed anyway and the Lord told me to wait. Not too long after, my husband confirmed what I didn't want to hear - I needed to wait. I was hurt, but I knew that since it was God's plan for me to go back to school, his plan (including his timing) would prevail.

As the months progressed and I heard from friends in grad school, I felt stupid. I was married, with child, had a college degree and no career. On the other hand, my friends were furthering their educations, so that they could establish themselves in a career and become the self-made people that the world respected and admired. Boy, did the world succeed in implanting that carnal seed in my mind! At the time, I didn't really know that a career would cause me to gain the respect that I was seeking; but it was the fear of the Lord that would garner it.

Day after day, I watched him go to work, beat the challenges, and excel - while I was at home nauseated and suffering from sinus headaches. I was happy about his rapid career advancement- But when would mine start? Despite my self pity, I prayed for him daily, praying for those in authority over him and thanking the Lord for the opportunities and the promotions.

But I was double-minded about this whole thing. One moment I was happy for him, the next moment I was envious because I wanted a career. I had contemplated the devil's lie that I was career less, for so long, until I was convinced that my husband thought I was stupid. So when he came home from work, I felt like he was belittling me when he asked questions or spoke to me.

One day, totally fed up with the perception that I thought he had of me, I asked him a question. "Do you think that I am stupid?, I am not some house wife that wakes up late, lays around watching soaps, and pampers herself all day!", I told him sternly. "I am not a house wife. I am not married to my house. I am a writer." He had no idea that I had been battling this false perception for several months. At this point, he began to make the connection between the false perception that I believed and my inconsistent attitude toward him.

As a loving husband, he reassured me, over and over and over again that he didn't think of me that way at all. He knew that I wasn't an idle, lazy, or selfish person. He also told me that he supported my going to grad school - but that he didn't consider it wise to go right then. Then, he began to tell me how he viewed me. He considered me to be capable of much more than I thought I was even capable of. I had no idea that he thought of me so highly.

I was relieved to know that he didn't view me as the devil convinced me to believe, but I still needed affirmation and encouragement about our future. I desperately wanted to know God's plan for me as the wife and mother of our new family. So, I kept studying and praying for direction.

First, I studied Sarah and Abraham since they were the patriarch and matriarch of faith, who had marital challenges but came out victorious. While studying Sarai's name, I found that her name means princess, yet it also means to be contentious and bossy. Now this was significant for at least 3 reasons:

- Princesses have favor because of who their fathers are
- Princesses often struggle through life not feeling esteemed as royalty and trying to prove their power and position
- Princesses who don't submit to the authority of their father, have the title without the privilege of power

Sarai had favor and the blessing of the Lord in her life because she chose God and not idols. His favor on her life was obvious. She had servants, wealth and riches. The Bible also tells us that she was a beautiful woman, yet barren. She probably lived a life feeling as if she was neither valued nor esteemed by her husband. His attempts to pass her off as his sister, due to fear, and her lack of ability to have children probably kept her at an all time low.

So, she struggled for 9 decades trying to prove her power and position as a woman of God. Yet she still remained barren. To get Abraham's attention, she used her emotions to persuade and to manipulate his behavior in her favor. Though her name meant princess, she probably wondered why she wasn't treated like one. She probably felt powerless. She chose the Lord as her God, but she wasn't fully submitted to Him because of what she felt He hadn't done for her. When He sent his angels to give Word about her future pregnancy, she laughed. Her cynicism toward his Word, tells us that she wasn't fully submitted to him. She felt that she had lived this way for so long, her situation couldn't change. But God had a plan for her life.

Genesis 17:15
> *And God said unto Abraham, As for Sarai thy wife,*
> *thou shalt not call her name Sarai, but Sarah shall*
> *her name be.*

Now Sarah was not just a princess, but her husband was told to call her "noblewoman". Her new name emphasized the necessary adaptation of godly qualities and attributes. She didn't change overnight, but her name did. God caused her husband to call her what God intended for her to become.

During this time, the Holy Spirit revealed some life-changing things to me:

1. God would cause my husband to esteem me as a noble woman
2. It didn't have to take 90 years
3. I had to fully submit to the Lord and let The Word shape my character

1 Peter 3:6

> *It was thus that Sarah obeyed Abraham [following his guidance and acknowledging his headship over her by] calling him lord (master, leader, authority). And you are now her true daughters if you do right and let nothing terrify you [not giving way to hysterical fears or letting anxieties unnerve you].*

I had a choice to make; I could either be Sarai or Sarah. I could continue to be a powerless princess in waiting, or I could become noble like God designed me to be. The characteristics of a noble person are: righteousness, graciousness, fearlessness and unselfishness. Sarah wasn't born this way; she had to work on her character. As Sarah, I had to forsake the world's way, the carnal way, the fleshly way; and do God's will.

I had to stop struggling with worldly wisdom that told me to be in charge and I had to acknowledge my husband as the one God held responsible for leading our household. Then, I had to trust that the Lord would do what he said that he would do – give me a future and a hope in my marriage and household. Though I didn't call my husband lord, like Sarah, I submitted to God by not rebelling against the natural authority that God placed over me.

I wanted to be praised like the woman in Proverbs 31. I knew that that woman's husband praised her. But, I looked at her character. Her character is what her husband praised. He praised those attributes that looked like the character of Christ Jesus. He didn't praise her flesh. She was called excellent, virtuous, and noble.

I wanted my husband to esteem me as a noblewoman, so I began to work on my attitude. I worked on crucifying my flesh. I began to adapt the skills and character traits befitting of a dignified and noblewoman. As I began to allow the Lord to minister to me about myself, I began to change. I don't know how long it took. It really didn't matter. All I know is that through my obedience and submission to the Lord, God gave him divine direction to rename me; to see me as a noblewoman.

It was as if God let my husband see me through His eyes. My husband began to go out of his way to meet my needs and give me those things that blessed me. He talked to me differently, with more respect and honor. He spent extra time learning what I liked and didn't like, what I ate and didn't eat, what made me laugh and what didn't make me laugh. He began openly discussing his respect for me and esteem for me as his wife. He wanted to make me feel like a princess and he did.

WISE WOMEN GET ATTENTION

Proverbs 31:30, 31

> *Charm and grace are deceptive, and beauty is vain [because it is not lasting], but a woman who reverently and worshipfully fears the Lord, she shall be praised! Give her the fruit of her hands, and let her own works praise her in the gates [of the city].*

God placed within each woman an appetite to be noticed and attended to. Every wife wants her husband to creatively and consistently meet her desires and needs. But to many women, this concept is just a fantasy. Attention is something that every woman wants, some crave, and few get.

The Old Testament gives us many examples of carnal women who did anything to get attention. And each time it was the anything that got them into trouble. Some say that Bathsheba wanted David's attention. She wanted it so much that she bathed on the rooftop facing David's palace, but the incident produced death for her husband and her illegitimate baby. Delilah craved attention. She flirted, flattered, enticed, and deceived Samson, but the end result for her was probably death when his last feat of strength destroyed over 3000 Philistines.

The strange (fornicating, cunning, adulterous) woman, who is described numerous times in the book of Proverbs, craved attention too. She flatters with her smooth speech, she dresses herself in ways that will lure a man, and she ultimately desires for his soul to be consumed with desire for her. But in the end the Bible says that she is ignorant and destined for death.

Though many of these women wanted or craved attention, none of them received the attention that fulfilled them. They got nothing shy of being noticed. Not one of these women had a supernatural testimony about how the Lord blessed them with a husband, but they all shared one common ending – destruction.

Even today, things haven't changed. Here are 10 carnal ways that women are dying to get a man's attention:

1. Wear provocative clothing (showing cleavage, midriffs, a lot of skin)
2. Excessive use of make-up, hair and nails
3. Flirting and teasing
4. Be open, blunt, and sexually frank about their past and future relationships
5. Compromise beliefs (being rebellious)
6. Exalt self and their personal life (job, car, house, schooling, etc.)
7. Be more daring (act more spontaneously)
8. Plan to be naughty (let defenses down via alcohol, etc.)
9. Vulgar, suggestive dancing
10. Spend money on them

Even Christian wives utilize these and other carnal methods of getting their husband's attention. But none of these things are productive in a marriage relationship, instead they are counter-productive. They are vain actions void of any lasting fulfillment. The Bible says that marriage is to be held in honor among all (Heb. 13:4). These methods are dishonorable, worldly, and they bring glory to self and not God.

If these tactics established a blessed marriage and household, these women would be happily married, fulfilled mothers, praising the Lord and being blessed by their husbands. But instead, we see hopeless women given into excess concerning the adorning of their bodies, attitudes, and emotions, and tired of trying what the world told them will work.

The world strives for attention. They compete with others for it, they fight for it. But attention is something that we (Christians) should not strive for, it is to be earned. When a woman of God strives for attention, she will never be fulfilled. Striving for attention will catapult a marriage onto a path of destruction.

At one time or another, every wife has felt like they needed to steal their husband's attention away from something: television, buddies, sporting events, or his job. However, in an effort not to lose him to these things, some women begin fighting for their relationships and end up fighting their husbands. They use their mouths as a weapon as they lash out at him and everything that pertains to him. Although many wives are looking for meaningful communication and affirmation, some will settle for negative attention (yelling & fussing).

I know this to be personally true. When my husband and I first married, we began to have problems communicating to each other clearly (candidly and free from sarcasm). The only thing that we could do peacefully together was pray. If we talked about anything else, it almost always ended up in an argument. When he watched TV, I became insulted that it could get his attention more than me, his wife, who was actually in the room with him.

It angered me so much because he watched TV so that he wouldn't have to communicate with me. So I fought for his attention. First I started out by trying to get him to watch what I wanted, getting his attention off of the shows that I considered stupid. Then, a couple of times I actually unplugged the television when he wasn't fully communicating with me. When that didn't work to my liking, I told him that I wasn't going to wash his clothes and I would cook the meals that I liked.

All of these things just added to his lack of ability to properly communicate with me. If the Lord hadn't shown me my wicked ways, I would have ended up striving for attention, lacking communication, void of fulfillment, and in route for a separation. When God showed me that the way that I operated was fleshly and wicked, I had to change. I could not rationalize why I did what I did. I had to accept the Lord's loving chastisement and reject the enemy's persuasion that I was condemning myself.

I had to allow God to be honest with me. Then, I had to be honest with him. He told me that I didn't fear him. Fear of the Lord was the key to the dignity, honor and respect that the Prov. 31 received. Virtuous women are rare. I had to decide whether I was going to be a dime a dozen, or one in a million.

I had to engraft the principles of God into my life. I couldn't perpetrate like I had everything under control, when I felt like I couldn't stand my husband. I couldn't be religious by going to church and praising God with the Body, but at home doing half of what God told me to do. I had to believe that God had a plan for my marriage and household, no matter how uncomfortable killing my flesh was. I had to fully submit to the Word of God, even the parts that I didn't like or seemed to difficult to me.

I purposed to live by the Word. As a result, my husband began to notice me. He began to watch me. When I walked into the room, he stopped what he was doing and would take notice. He looked for me and then greeted me when he came home from work. He noticed when I changed my hair, nails, and conversation. He complimented my use of godly wisdom and the Word. He not only noticed me, but he admired me.

NEEDING TO BE WANTED – WANTING TO BE NEEDED

Recently, I was looking through a magazine that showcased hairstyles. In it, there was a full page picture of about 6 women sitting under the hairdryer in throne-like beauty salon chairs. Each one of the women had a young, sensual, highly muscular, loin cloth wearing, bare foot and bare chest man bowing at their feet, which were perched upon a pedestal.

The look on each woman's face was one of sheer relaxation, delight and a strange sense of satisfaction as the men bowed to serve them. Though this depiction was nothing more than a carnal fantasy, it expressed the inner thoughts of many women (married, unmarried, Christian and non-Christian alike). That thought says: I need to be wanted. I want to be needed.

However, God did not create man to worship woman. Neither did he create husband to worship wife. But, the Bible does command the husband to dwell with her according to knowledge, to love her like he loves himself, and to treat her with gentleness and kindness in love. If we want what God wants for us, we've got to dump the non-realistic, fantasy inspired idea of being worshipped.

Common Scenario #1:

You, a Christian woman marries a man who appears to have it going on. He has a good job, money invested, his future planned, is nicely dressed, well manicured, intelligent, strong, physically fit, highly respected, thoughtful, well-spoken, rising up the ladder of success and walking in the Word. He isn't a leech, but is in control and independent. He lives his life at what looks like a high level of success. After marrying him you enjoy the triumphant times with him, while together praying through the challenging ones.

Yet, through it all he always seems to have an answer for every situation. Since he is the head, he has to give an answer. He is accountable to God for the household. He hears your insight, but often knows what direction he wants to go in beforehand. Eventually the thought, in whatever form, pops up in your mind: I know he loves me, but does he need me?

Many years ago, those were my sentiments. Even though I knew that my husband loved me, I didn't feel like I was needed. I wanted for the Lord to show me in His word where a wise woman is needed in her husband's life, not just wanted. After much prayer and quiet time with the Lord, He gave me four characteristics that made me priceless to him. Every wise woman's husband needs: her stewardship, her integrity, her encouragement, and her strength.

He Needs Your Stewardship
Stewardship is the ability to manage household affairs in excellence

Proverbs 31:11 (Amplified)
> *The heart of her husband trusts in her confidently and relies on and believes in her securely, so that he has no lack of [honest] gain or no need of [dishonest] spoil.*

In High Schools around this country, there was a time where all young ladies had the opportunity to take Home Economics as an elective. Many biased counselors around the country told young girls like me, "You don't need to take home economics. That's for kids who aren't very smart. That's for kids who want an easy A. That's for kids who want to lollygag. You are too smart for that."

I attended a very good high school in an affluent community in Southeast Texas. In my heart I was interested in taking home economics. My mother took it, my grandmother had a college degree in it - I thought it would be interesting. However, as I walked down the hallway glancing into the home ec room, I began to think that the counselor was right.

As I peeked in, I saw young girls who were braiding each other's hair, playing chase around the room and flirting with the few boys who were in there. None of the honors students or average students were in that class. Needless to say, I forgot about it as quickly as I thought about it.

I was blessed to have a mother who loved being a mother. She allowed me to cook, taught me to clean, hand sew, and groom myself. I admired and attentively watched my mother do everything. As a result, I became interested in arts and crafts, interior decorating, cooking, managing money, etc. Because many women didn't have a female role model, who modeled excellence in motherhood or wifedom, many today are struggling between working outside of the home and working in the home.

I hear women say that they don't know what they would do if they were a "stay at home" mom. They weren't so interested in the home skills that their mothers had. When they had the opportunity to learn in school, they dismissed it as a blow-off class. Society placed little value on home building skills and more on career skills - to the detriment of many.

The essence of a home economics class is to teach proper stewardship over a household. The Greek word for stewardship is oikonomia {oy-kon-om-ee-ah}. It means to manage household or household affairs. From it, we get the English words economy and economist. Wise women learn, with the wisdom and insight of God, and then implement a combination of three things. First, we need to learn about economy as it relates to the household. Economics deals with:

- budgeting
- production
- distribution

Second, we need to be home economists. Economists are those who are dedicated to learning the most efficient and expedient ways to save money, prevent waste of food or material things, develop and adhere to a budget, and develop systems to deal with, produce and distribute material or physical needs. In other words, they become experts in the home field.

The wise woman's husband in Proverbs 31 needed for his wife to be a good oikonomia (home economist). The Bible says that he was a man that was known in the city gates, while sitting with the elders of the land. This man was busy working, probably away from home quite a bit. He needed to know that he could trust her to handle the household finances so that they could continue to accumulate wealth and not have to dishonestly gain to pay off debt. If we want our husbands to need us, we too must be excellent home administrators/managers.

Your husband needs you to be an excellent administrator of household affairs. That is not to say that *you* need to do all of the work that needs to be done. However, a good manager delegates responsibility to others, even if those others are hired. Your husband needs to know that the household is operating smoothly whether he is there or not. He doesn't need for you to call him 10 hours a day with every pressing situation that you encounter.

When he sees that you can and will manage the home in excellence, he can demonstrate more diligence on his job. His attentions will then fully focus on the task at hand, not the situation at home. He will learn more and show forth enough diligence for the Lord to see to it that he has favor with his employer and a raise/promotion in his near future. As a result, his advancement becomes your advancement. The household is blessed when you seek the Lord for revelation on how to properly manage your home.

He Needs Your Integrity
Integrity is the quality or state of being unimpaired

Proverbs 31:16 (Amplified)
> *She considers a [new] field before she buys or accepts it [expanding prudently and not courting neglect of her present duties by assuming other duties]; with her savings [of time and strength] she plants fruitful vines in her vineyard.*

When we think of the word integrity, we think of things like honesty, truthfulness, and moral soundness. However the definition that I want to focus on right now is one that many don't consider when they talk about this characteristic in a Believer's life. Integrity is the quality or state of being unimpaired. Your husband needs you to be unimpaired. Let me give you an example.

People who have an inability to hear correctly due to damage of the ear drums, ear canal, or hearing organs are considered hearing impaired. Instead of hearing fully and wholly like many of us, the quality of their hearing is lessened by some sort of damage. Their ears are not whole. They work in part, if at all. Essentially, the integrity of their hearing is hindered by some sort of damage.

When a man's wife is damaged, she is not whole. When we have not gotten rid of the scars of past relationships, past failures, past hurts or fears - we are damaged. When we have not repented from carnal methods of doing things, harbored unforgiveness, bitterness or resentment - we are damaged. Our integrity, our ability to minister from a state of wholeness is lessened, weakened, even strained when we are in this state.

Therefore, we can't function the way that God created us to function. Ultimately, God wants us to worship him with a whole heart. Not a heart torn, worn, beaten, and hardened. He wants us to be whole. If we will let the Word of God minister to us and then do what God tells us to do (obey it) then the Lord will begin to restore us. Jehovah Rapha, God our healer, doesn't want to patch up the wounds of your heart, but he wants to heal them and restore you to a state of wholeness.

Your husband needs you to be whole. He needs you to lay aside every weight that easily besets you. He needs you to be fearless, forgiving, and not easily offended. He needs you to uncompromisingly follow God's word, seek his face, and go forth in the joy of the Lord.

When you are whole, your integrity is in tact. You can go forth unrestricted by past damages or injuries. You can minister to the needs of your family without apprehension and in the soundness of the mind of Christ. Your husband can count on you to make sound decisions and sound judgment, knowing that you walk in the strength of God's word.

Let me stop here for a moment. Some of you may be wondering why should you try to be all that or do all of this when your husband isn't living right, let alone being a Believer. My answer to you is simple. You are doing this all AS UNTO THE LORD anyhow.

He Needs Your Encouragement

Proverbs 31:12 (Amplified)
She comforts, encourages, and does him only good as long as there is life within her.
To encourage means to empower with courage

When I married my husband, he was already successful in his career, strong in the Lord, and unwavering in diligence, discipline, and self control. He always seemed to have a strong sense of who he was in the Lord. He was so confident in his relationship with

God and in what He would do in his life, that others perceived him to be a little arrogant. Eventually I did too.

I loved him, but because I thought that he was so sure of himself, he didn't need my encouragement. Instead, I opted for the easier task, prayer. I prayed for him daily, but there comes a time when praying for your husband is not enough. I am not diminishing the power of God to do a work in his life or situation, but the wise woman in Proverbs 31 probably encouraged her husband.

Compliments won't cut it. He needs to be encouraged. To encourage means to give courage to. Courage is the capacity to meet danger without giving into fear. The wise woman has the ability to give courage to her husband. She has the ability to help her husband face the challenges in his life without giving into fear, by giving him the Word of God.

No matter how much you may perceive your husband to be a self-motivated man. No matter how much he encourages himself in the Lord, he still needs you. Your husband needs your encouragement. He needs for you to speak the Word of God over him and into his life. The Bible shows us that when Jesus was tempted, he spoke the Word and the devil fled. When we speak the Word over our spouses, we release the power of God over his life and the Lord then redirects his mind to the promises and not the problems. As a result, he can press on and be a blessing to the family.

He Needs Your Strength
Strength is the ability to resist attack

Proverbs 31:25 (Amplified)
> *Strength and dignity are her clothing and her position is strong and secure; she rejoices over the future [the latter day or time to come, knowing that she and her family are in readiness for it]!*

Common Scenario #2
Your husband has an opportunity to do a job assignment, created specifically for his advancement. The company has his eyes on your man, no one else. This job will give him high visibility

within the company and will prepare him for a position that is highly esteemed and coveted. It requires an intense 6 month training position, in which he will work later hours and travel out of town to attend leadership development courses. If he does well, he will be promoted and receive a raise well beyond the norm.

But, he can't do it alone. He needs your strength. One definition of strength is the ability to resist attack. Your husband needs for you to stand your ground firmly and resist the attack of the enemy, the devil. As soon as your husband goes on this assignment, the attacks will come. The enemy will attack: your marriage, your faith, your trust, your peace/rest and your sleep.

The weapon of choice is to be the Word of God. The Bible says that if we submit to God, we can resist the devil and he will flee. Your husband needs for you to be submitted to the Word, not just knowledgeable of it - but walking in it. He needs for you to be able to speak the Word of God, when the spirit of fear comes to frighten you while your husband is out of town. He needs for you to confess the Word when the enemy tells you that his employer is just doggin' him. Ultimately, God needs for you to believe and confess His Word even when you feel like your husband is not meeting your needs.

The wise woman of God walks in the strength of God's Word. She doesn't complain, murmur or harbor false suspicion. She doesn't need her husband to sit by her side as she prays out to the Lord. She has her own relationship with Him. She knows how to hear from him and apply his Word as she stands her ground to resist the attack of the enemy. Neither is she worried whether she will be richly rewarded for her acts of kindness and many expressions of love. She is content in knowing that these things are necessary in order for her to be an excellent wife, mother, businesswoman and teacher.

PART 5

WISDOM AT WORK

WHAT WISDOM LOOKS LIKE

Proverbs 9:10
> *The fear of the LORD is the beginning of wisdom,*
> *And the knowledge of the Holy One is understanding.*

Imagine this: You are cooking some rice on the stove and it will be ready in 15 minutes. So, you figure that you can do a couple of things and then come back and tend to the rice. However, when you return, the water has boiled out, the air is full of smoke, and the house smells like burnt rice. You desperately want to get out and breathe in the fresh air. If you can open a window or a door, you can get the fresh air in and the polluted air out.

The door is like the fear of the Lord. It is the opening that will bring you into the wisdom of God. If you will believe that it is the Lord who will deliver you from the smoky house and then seek Him, you are on your way to becoming a wise woman.

The word wisdom consists of two smaller words: wise and dominion. When a Believer walks in the wisdom of God, she draws from and uses God's vast and infinite knowledge and skill to govern or master her world.

She no longer relies upon carnal or fleshly methods of operation, but solely relies upon the wisdom of the Lord to help build her house. Now, in order to successful build, there are at least 5 things that the woman of God must do with the wisdom of God. She must: recognize it, ask for it, attain it, use it, and store it.

Recognize it
James 3:17

> *But the wisdom that is from above is first pure, then peaceable, gentle, and easy to be intreated, full of mercy and good fruits, without partiality, and without hypocrisy.*

This scripture clearly illustrates wisdom's traits. When the woman of God recognizes these 7 qualities in the life a mature Believer, she has seen the wisdom of God at work.

GOD'S WISDOM IS:

1. Pure - God's infinite knowledge and skills are untainted and uninfluenced by man's finite perception of life. God didn't need and doesn't need our input on how to do anything. His wisdom is faultless. Therefore, fleshly actions/attitudes can't be rationalized, when the wisdom of God is at work.

2. Peacable - (peace + able) The wisdom of God can bring peace (security, safety, tranquility and prosperity).

3. Gentle - The wisdom of God is temperate.

4. Easy to be entreated - God's wisdom brings about a willingness to obey his Word.

5. Full of mercy & good fruits - God's wisdom brings about a kindness, desire, willingness to help those around who are in distress. It also produces productive, profitable, and effective endeavors/work.

6. Without partiality - God's wisdom doesn't accuse, rationalize, discriminate, contend, or strive with others.

7. Without hypocrisy - God's wisdom doesn't impersonate, pretend, or act fake. Wise women don't say one thing and do another or give someone else biblical counsel, but don't heed it for themselves.

Ask for it

James 1:5

> *If any of you lack wisdom, let him ask of God, that giveth tó all men liberally, and upbraideth not; and it shall be given him.*

If we ask for wisdom, God will give it to us freely, but it isn't free. In order to obtain the wisdom of God, you must do some work. What is actually wisdom from God starts out as information to us. At first, our minds perceive the Word and it's principles as divine information. The principles and counsel of the Lord are His wisdom. But we must activate the wisdom of God in our lives through obedience to the Word.

Acquire it & Use it

Proverbs 4:7

> *Wisdom is the principal thing; therefore get wisdom: and with all thy getting get understanding.*

Many people have gained wisdom, but they are void of understanding. They memorize a zillion scriptures, but obey few of them. They may even teach the Word, but they don't obey what they teach. They have the Word, biblical principles, godly counsel - but they lack understanding. They really don't know how God works in their lives. Yet they can see what God does in others lives.

Therefore, getting understanding is a necessary step in acquiring wisdom. Understanding is the revelation that comes as a result of doing God's word, obeying his commandments and following his principles.

When you make up your mind to do the will of God, you may not know how he is going to work everything out. You may not even know how your obedient actions are going to change the situation, because you simply want to obey.

However, once you've been obedient to the Word, look with expectancy for supernatural manifestation. Once you experience the power of God's word in your life, so that you begin to see change and reconstruction, then you will start to understand and intimately relate to the importance of obedience to the Word.

Store it

Proverbs 2:10-13

> *When wisdom enters your heart, And knowledge is*
>   *pleasant to your soul,*
> *Discretion will preserve you; Understanding will*
>   *keep you,*
> *To deliver you from the way of evil, From the man*
>   *who speaks perverse things,*
> *From those who leave the paths of uprightness To*
>   *walk in the ways of darkness;*

This scripture contains an awesome promise from the Word of God concerning wisdom and knowledge, but there are 2 things that we must do. First, we must let wisdom enter into our hearts. Many Believers let wisdom enter into their minds, but they don't meditate, study, or obey the Word of God. The heart is the treasure chest in which we store God's word. It is where we put those things that are most dear and valuable to us.

Second, knowledge has to become pleasant to our souls. The way that we receive knowledge is through processing information, which is learning. That means we must sincerely desire and become comfortable with learning God's way of doing things. The main way that we can become comfortable is by doing them. It takes some practice.

Life Example

At the beginning of each year, I ask the Lord to show me a couple of things that I can do to be a more excellent wife & mother. I am asking for knowledge. I want to know something that I didn't know before, that will help me to serve better. I don't ask God for an exhaustive list, I'm sure that I could become overwhelmed. I ask him for a couple of things that I work on ALL year long.

When I first started doing this, it was a little difficult because some of the things that I had to do seemed simple and others seemed difficult. I had to work at crucifying my flesh in many areas just to accomplish one of those tasks. But when I saw the results 1 year later, I was delighted. Knowledge became pleasant to my soul. By the end of the year, I was a different person. God was pleased and I was pleased to see how it brought joy to my family. So when we esteem the Word of God as valuable treasure to obey and then practice doing things God's way, we can't go wrong.

There are many examples of women in the Word, who established their homes according to God's specifications. They lay aside the fleshly way of doing things and functioned with the mind of Christ. In the next portion of this book, we will examine the lives of women who allowed God to build their homes and not the wisdom of the world. It is interesting to note that the examples that will be examined, illustrate women who have also overcome many of the same/similar mental, emotional and actual obstacles in their marriages and family lives. As you read, let the wisdom of God minister to your heart and produce great fruit in your life.

WISE WOMEN BUILDERS

Esther - Book of Esther

In the next several pages, I want to focus on some characteristics that wise women possessed in establishing their homes in excellence. You will need to read the book of Esther if you aren't already familiar with her story.

Synopsis

Esther's cousin Mordecai was an honorable and wise man, which adopted the young orphan and raised her as his own daughter. This man had the seemingly difficult task of raising her even though she had the potential to be rebellious, mean-spirited, or even bitter. He could've been like other men in his time, not handling his daughter with respect and honor, but he wasn't. His relationship with the Lord was first and foremost in raising this young woman. As his daughter, Esther was given instructions and life directions with the expectation that she would obey them. It had to be his walk with the Lord that caused her to respect her cousin and obey him as a father.

She obeyed wise counsel

When the King sought a new wife Esther was chosen above all of the other women. The Bible tells us that she was beautiful, lovely and highly favored. Yet in the midst of all of this favor and royal treatment, Esther could've let her flesh take control. She probably knew that she was on the road to becoming queen, but that didn't hinder her obedience to her father.

Esther 2:10

> *Esther had not revealed her people or family, for Mordecai had charged her not to reveal it.*

Just 10 verses later when Esther became queen, she didn't allow her new royal position cause her to get a big head or to become controlling. She could've acted like a "diva", but she didn't. She stayed obedient.

Esther 2:20

> *Now Esther had not revealed her family and her people, just as Mordecai had charged her, for Esther obeyed the command of Mordecai as when she was brought up by him.*

She Feared the Lord

Though the queen had much delegated authority, she stayed humble and submitted to God as she learned in her childhood. Even when one of the king's men plotted to kill her people, she requested that her maidens and Mordecai join her in a fast. Once the fast ended, then she approached her husband with the critical matter. This is a woman who knew how to reverence the Lord and obtain favor with her husband. Throughout this book, her husband tells her on numerous occasions that he would give half his kingdom to her, if she wanted it.

Yet, she didn't use the power and influence first and foremost. She knew that the power and favor of God was even greater than her position in the kingdom. Once she got before the Lord and submitted the situation to him, she would be empowered to submit to her husband the impending slaughter of her people. In return, God could then minister to her husband and extend more favor toward her and her people.

She submitted to her husband (as unto the Lord)

According to the customs of the times, the queen wasn't supposed to go in unto the king. To go in unto the king, meant to bow to him - to show an act of submission like the inhabitants of the kingdom. Instead, the law probably allowed her to just go to him with a matter as one who has as much authority as he does. But, she was willing to go against customs, against what was deemed acceptable to all, by choosing to humble herself before the Lord and then to submit to his authority over her – her husband.

Fasting allowed her to focus on the Lord and his power, not on her fear or her flesh. So, when she went to her husband to seek his favor of saving her people, she had been in God's presence. Therefore, she didn't run to him crying. Neither did she manipulate his authority. Instead, she calmly submitted her situation to him. As a matter of fact, she had so much self-control, she didn't even tell him right away. She waited until the next day.

Esther 4:16

Go, gather together all the Jews that are present in

Shushan, and fast ye for me, and neither eat nor drink three days, night or day: I also and my maidens will fast likewise; and so will I go in unto the king, which is not according to the law: and if I perish, I perish.

When she said if I die, I die, she didn't firmly believe that she would die. It was as if she was saying, once I submit it to God, obtain his wisdom, and walk in it, then I've done all that I can do. If after doing all of those things they want to kill me or I die, so be it.

Of course she didn't perish, but went on to obtain even greater favor from her husband, saved kingdom households from destruction, salvation for the Jewish people, a promotion for Mordecai, and she inherited the house of Haman, their enemy.

Hannah - 1 Samuel

You may be familiar with the story of Hannah. She was a barren woman who was married to a man who had another wife besides herself. Even though she was the more highly favored wife, Hannah's marriage had a myriad of problems. As if being barren, yet desperately wanting another child weren't enough, the other wife regularly humiliated her because of her barrenness.

Hannah lived in continual anguish, sadness, and maybe even depression over the fact that the other wife taunted her and flaunted her children before her. It seems as if Hannah lived a complicated life. However, it's not much different from the lives that many women of God live now. Though polygamy isn't widespread, there are many women who are married to men who have ex-wives and their children to deal with. The fact is that these women often try to make marriage to the new wife difficult and frustrating, while giving unnecessary and irrational parental responsibilities to the new couple.

She feared the Lord & Obeyed wise counsel
The Word tells us that Hannah was married to a man who

worshipped God and gave yearly sacrificial offerings. Each year, he would give the first wife and her children some of the sacrifice. But the Bible says that Hannah's portion was fixed. He loved her more, even though she was barren.

Each year that they went up to sacrifice, the other wife would ridicule, demean, and tease her for her inability to have children. She vexed Hannah to the point of tears and a loss of appetite. Not knowing how the wicked wife had verbally tortured Hannah, her husband asks her why she's so upset when she's been provided for in such a thorough way. She could've gone ballistic on him, for his insensitivity.

Of all people, he should've known her ups and downs, issues and all. But Hannah doesn't go off on him - like some Believers do when they get in the flesh. So instead of giving her husband a piece of her mind, she respects him as the head of the house, while telling the Lord all that is in her heart. Then she petitions the Lord for a son that she promises to dedicate to Him for the rest of his life.

Then, the priest sees her praying (without hearing the words come out of her mouth), accuses her of being drunk, and rebukes her for it. At this point, she could get in the flesh, like a lot of Believers would - but she chooses not to. Instead, look at what she said:

Submitted to the Authority of God

1 Samuel 1:15-16
> *And Hannah answered and said, No, my lord, I am a woman of a sorrowful spirit: I have drunk neither wine nor strong drink, but have poured out my soul before the LORD.*
> *Count not thine handmaid for a daughter of Belial: for out of the abundance of my complaint and grief have I spoken hitherto.*

She called the priest lord, a symbol signifying the respect for her spiritual elder. Then she told him her issue and let him know that she wasn't a daughter of an evil or lawless person who would come into the house of the Lord and disrespect it.

Her response to the priest was key. Immediately upon staying out of the flesh, she gained favor with the priest and he got in faith with her and spoke a blessing of favor and agreement about her petition to the Lord.

1 Samuel 1:17
> *Then Eli answered and said, Go in peace: and the God of Israel grant thee thy petition that thou hast asked of him.*

The Lord granted her petition. She had a son, Samuel. Being a woman of integrity, she kept her vow with the Lord. When Samuel was weaned, she and her husband offered a sacrifice, and took him to see the priest so that he could see the manifestation of her prayer and petition. In the end, she not only had 1 son, but 4 other children.

1 Samuel 2:21
> *And the LORD visited Hannah, so that she conceived, and bare three sons and two daughters. And the child Samuel grew before the LORD.*

Hannah chose not to create mass strife, confusion, and all out drama with the contentious wife. Neither did she choose to get into it with her husband about his apparent ignorance of her situation. Instead, she took her issues to the Lord. She trusted him and his word and the Lord empowered her to build her house.

Excellent wife - Proverbs 31:10-31

The Bible gives us many examples of wise women and the favor that they obtained from Him. Yet Proverbs 31 provides one of the most vivid descriptions of a wise woman's victorious life and abundantly blessed lifestyle.

Each time a Believer reads this chapter, they hope to have an abundantly blessed lifestyle like the wise woman in Proverbs 31, but Hope is not enough. Nick naming each other "virtuous woman" is not enough. We must endeavor to understand who this woman was, what she did, and how she prospered in life. Though none of us knows her name, we can all agree that she was a wise woman of God whose household and businesses esteemed, valued and blessed her.

Over a decade ago, I sought the Lord concerning this nameless woman. I desired to be her, but I didn't know how. One of the first things the Lord revealed to me was that this woman was not born this way. She didn't come into the world perfect and excellent. She had to work on herself. So, if I wanted her results – I had to work on myself. She had to learn to effectively manage herself before she could effectively manage anything or anyone else.

The Bible says that when we are good stewards over the little things, God will give us more.

The woman in Proverbs 31 was a woman of great responsibility and awesome stewardship. She didn't just start running things at the onset of her marriage. Neither did she have every skill necessary to become who God wanted her to be, but she adopted these skills along the way.

Look at it this way - She was not born excellent, she *became* excellent. At some point in her life she made the decision to be the best at what she did. Many of us look at this passage and try to claim this type of lifestyle or blessed home state, but we don't take the time to align our thoughts, beliefs, conversation, and actions with the Word of God. All of these things take time and the renewing of our minds to what the Word of God says about us and our lives.

As you read further, take some time and meditate the scriptures and revelation that God gave me as I set out to understand this woman in Proverbs 31.

Proverbs 31: 10-31

10 An excellent wife, who can find? For her worth is far above jewels.
She is capable, intelligent, virtuous, rare.

11 The heart of her husband trusts in her, And he will have no lack of gain.
She is trustworthy and reliable

12 She does him good and not evil All the days of her life.
She is comforting, encouraging, submitted to him
AS UNTO THE LORD

13 She looks for wool and flax, And works with her hands in delight.
She is diligent and joyful in her work

14 She is like merchant ships; She brings her food from afar.
She is resourceful and dedicated to purpose..

15 She rises also while it is still night, And gives food to her household, And portions to her maidens.
She is focused and manages her household well.

16 She considers a field and buys it; From her earnings she plants a vineyard.
She gathers knowledge and makes wise decisions and sows from her harvest.

17 She girds herself with strength, And makes her arms strong.
She is strong mentally and physically. Exercise is a way of life..

18 She senses that her gain is good; Her lamp does not go out at night.
She concerns herself with pleasing God - Woman of faith - the Word of God is an ever present lamp that burns within her.

19 She stretches out her hands to the distaff, And her hands grasp the spindle.
She is diligent.

20 She extends her hand to the poor; And she stretches out her hands to the needy.
She is compassionate and merciful and her life is one of ministry.

21 She is not afraid of the snow for her household, For all her household are clothed with scarlet.
She is a woman who walks by faith and holds fast to the blood covenant.

22 She makes coverings for herself; Her clothing is fine linen and purple.
She is creative; Her clothing exemplifies her strong and dignified character.

23 Her husband is known in the gates, When he sits among the elders of the land.
Her husband is a man of integrity, diligence and great skill (Proverbs 22:29).

24 She makes linen garments and sells *them,* And supplies belts to the tradesmen.
She is an entrepreneur who uses her gifts in business.

25 Strength and dignity are her clothing, And she smiles at the future.
She is strong in the Lord, He is the lifter of her head, and she is assured of his faithfulness to her and her family.

26 She opens her mouth in wisdom, And the teaching of kindness is on her tongue.
She exercises skillful and Godly wisdom in her words and actions. She is gracious.

27 She looks well to the ways of her household, And

does not eat the bread of idleness.
Her highest calling is that of taking care of her family, so she doesn't neglect them in any way.

30 Charm is deceitful and beauty is vain, *But* a woman who fears the LORD, she shall be praised. *Above all, the most important thing in her life is to do the will of God.*

Capable
Intelligent
Virtuous
Rare
Trustworthy
Reliable
Comforting
Encouraging
Submitted
Diligent In Her Career/Work
Joyful
Resourceful
Focused
Good Home Manager
Wise
Sower
Athletic
Walks By Faith
Holds Fast To The Promises Of God/Blood Covenant
Compassionate
Merciful
Purposeful
Clothing Reflects Her Character
Kind
Household Is First Priority
Diligent In Ministry To Family
Fears The Lord

Above all, the distinguishing factor between the wise woman in Proverbs 31 and other women is that she feared the Lord. The blessings of fearing the Lord are riches, honor and an abundant life – all of which she enjoyed. She reverenced the Lord God and his word above all else. If the Word said to do xyz, then she did xyz. She infused godly principles into her life and walked in them on a daily basis and the Lord God increased her more and more!

Remember: Change doesn't happen over night. It happens over a period of time once consistency has occurred.

PRICELESS SKILLS OF A WISE WOMAN

Skill is the ability to do something well, but in order to do something well, you have to practice. You must do it over and over and over again until it becomes so much a part of you that you do it subconsciously. The good news here is that a wise woman isn't born wise. She often starts out a foolish woman who, in the midst of her turmoil, begins to search God's Word for knowledge on how to obtain a better marriage, personal life and family life.

Then, by consistently hearing the Word of God, her faith begins to grow. She starts to believe that God didn't make any mistakes and that she can be the wife God desires for her to be. Her relentless application of the Word to her situations coupled with the abandonment of worldly opinions produced a life of fulfillment and joy.

God's Building Model

In Exodus 35, God gives us the details of the building of his holy temple. In this example, we can see the importance of attitude and skill in building the most holy building ever erected on earth. First, Moses told the Israelites (under direct orders from God) to bring an offering to be used in the building of the temple.

Whoever had the ability to do something well, was asked to exercise their skill to help build. God had a list of things that he needed for them to use in the construction of the holy temple. However God made a point of saying that he would only receive an offering from those whose hearts were motivated and spirits willing to build.

Skill was so important in the building of the temple, that God anointed Bezalel with wisdom, intelligence, understanding, knowledge, and all craftsmanship. The Bible says that God put it in Bezalel's heart to teach others how to attain the skills necessary to create what the Lord desired in his temple.

Over a decade ago, the Lord motivated me to build according to His word. He gave me insight and revelation of the skills that I needed in order to build my household according to His specifications. I believe that the Lord has anointed me to teach these skills to the newly married, already married, and the unmarried.

In the next several pages, we are going to look at some of the priceless skills that a woman of God must learn, adapt, consistently apply and do well in. It is these characteristics that make the wise woman unique and distinctly different from others who only pretend to be virtuous.

Skill #1 - Prayer

Prayer is God's foolproof method to have and maintain peace.

Philippians 4:6-7

> *Be careful for nothing; but in every thing by prayer and supplication with thanksgiving let your requests be made known unto God. And the peace of God, which passeth all understanding shall keep your hearts and minds through Christ Jesus.*

Mark 11: 24,25 (Amplified)

> *. . . Whatever you ask for in prayer, believe (trust and be confident) that it is granted to you, and you will [get it].*

And whenever you stand praying, if you have anything against anyone, forgive him and let it drop (leave it, let it go) in order that your Father Who is heaven may also forgive you your [own] failings and shortcomings and let them drop.

Be anxious for nothing ~ Pray

When we hear the word anxious, we think of things like anxiety, worry, impatience, and fear. However, the word anxious is a derivative of the word distraction: dis: away tract: to draw ion: the state of. So in essence, God is actually commanding us to not let anything pull us or draw us away from His plan and toward our own agenda. The danger in this is that distractions can lead to a path of natural and or spiritual death. The Bible says that there is a way that seems right to a man, but the end is death (Prov. 14:12). (The way seems right to some because it's comfortable. It lines up with what the flesh wants to do.)

This principle is all throughout the word of God. Look at some of the distractions that lead to death natural or spiritual.

- Samson was distracted by Delilah. He died naturally.
- Eve was distracted by the Devil. She died spiritually.
- David was distracted by Bathsheba. The result of their sin ended in natural death for their baby.
- The men who were distracted by the strange woman in Proverbs were led to their spiritual deaths.

God's desire is that we stay focused. He wants for us to not be distracted by anyone or anything.

Proverbs 4:25-26

> *Let thine eyes look right on, and let thine eyelids look straight before thee.*
> *Ponder the path of thy feet, and let all thy ways be established.*

Many years ago, I had a desire that was so pressing that it almost distracted me from what the Lord had for my life. Months after I had just gotten married, I wanted to go home. I was over 2000 miles from home, and without a friend or relative. I didn't like our house, my new neighborhood looked depressing, the people in my new city were rude and ignorant, and the majority of them treated me like I was stupid. It wasn't like home (Texas).

Though I was in the situation, I wasn't afraid. Yet I was frustrated because my husband and I were so different that it was like night and day. What was funny to him didn't make me laugh. What excited him didn't excite me. He didn't want to talk about certain issues when I was ready to talk about them. Our communication patterns were totally out of sync. This isn't what I expected or wanted out of our marriage. I wasn't happy at all. I wanted to go home.

So that year, I went to Texas for about 2 months and I went home again in December for at least 1½ months. My husband would come with me and then he would fly back to go to work. I just needed to chill out, I thought. But, I was distracted.

God wanted my husband and I to work things out. He wanted us to learn how to function together as husband and wife. He wanted us to begin the process of coming together as one. He wanted us to walk together in agreement, even if it meant disagreeing with each other in love. But, I wanted out - temporarily.

Just like the theme song on the TV show, Cheers, I wanted to go where everyone knew my name and was always glad I came. I wanted to go where there were no troubles, but happy times. I allowed my desire to go back to my comfort zone (home) distract me from building the new home that God had given me.

The longer that I stayed away from my husband, the more I thought I had peace. At my parents home, there were no arguments, no bitterness, no uncomfortable expectations, no stubbornness, no unwilling giving up of myself. But one day the Lord began to show me that my distractions were going to have a profound effect on the outcome of my marriage. If I continued to go home for extended vacations without him, the communication that I was hoping would get better, would die. And that would just be the beginning.

I didn't want a divorce. I didn't want to be separated. Even though I thought about him while I was away, he got on my nerves when we were together. I had to pray; and I needed to do it differently than before. I had to stop second guessing God, as if he had made a mistake and gave me the wrong man. I had to pray in faith, believing that God would hear my cry and give me a revelation. He would intervene on our behalf and destroy the chaos, the confusion, the stubbornness, and the distractions.

Abiding in his Peace

So I began to pray differently. I didn't pray for the Lord to change him. Instead, I began to pray according to Phil. 4. I began to worship God for his goodness and thank him for giving me a man of God. I'll admit that it was difficult at first. But, the Lord led me to make a list of positive things about my husband and then I began to thank God for all of the godly attributes that he possessed. The more I thanked God for him, the more that I became excited in the Lord about this mighty man of God. I began to ask God to let me see him through his divine eyes - and he did.

God showed me my husband in the spirit - not the flesh. When I saw him, I saw him void of the things that irritated me. In the spirit, there are no idiosyncrasies or pet peeves. I saw him as a mighty man who honored God as Lord over his life. I saw a royal son of the Most High King. I saw him as a well groomed son that God loved, trained up and prepared to enter into a covenant with me.

As a result of the constant prayers of thanksgiving and the requests to God concerning my marriage, the second half of the scripture began to kick in. God's peace began to keep my heart and mind. From that point on, each time our relationship hit some rough spots, I first offered God thanksgivings and then requests and the peace of God kept my heart and mind away from the distractions and on the Lord's plan for my life as a married woman. The peace of God ministered "be still" to my heart and mind.

When my flesh wanted to start planning another "vacation", the Lord ministered "be still and know that I am God, I am in control." Once I allowed the peace of God to rule over my heart and mind, I didn't want to go back to my old way of thinking about the situation or doing what I did in the past.

In an effort to escape those things that you don't like about your husband, some of you have allowed yourselves to get distracted. You are distracted by spending, shopping, the phone, girl friends, or spending lots of time away from home. All of these things feed the tension, attitudes, lack of communication, and chaos at home. It is these small distractions that cause marriages to fail. But if you take the wisdom shared in this section, consistently apply it in your life, you will see the peace of God come into your midst and astound you. You will know that it is his peace that has kept you because he will intercede and you will choose not to do, think or say what you have in the past.

Skills # 2 & 3 - Submission & Humility

James 4:7
> *Therefore submit to God. Resist the devil and he will*
> *flee from you.*

Submission is a choice; it's not a dirty word. However in the context of marriage, most of us have (at one time or another) associated the "s" word with negative things. Those negative things were enough to repulse me from the concept of submission in my pre-adult life. As a result, my double mind told me that when I got married, I should love, yet I should function independent of the vision that my husband had for us.

I was a spirit-filled Believer, but my mind wasn't renewed to the biblical principle of submission. So, I believed that in being independent, I didn't need to be accountable to my husband in everything - just some things. I figured that if I wanted to do something, I could half submit. I could just tell my husband what I wanted to do, yet not allow his input may or may not affect my desires or decision. And if he didn't see things my way, I could persuade him to and eventually get what I wanted.

My disgust with the concept of submission was evident to my husband before we married. At one point in our engagement period, we began to discuss several issues that we could face as a newly married couple to determine if we saw eye to eye on them. In the midst of discussing one, we began to argue. While arguing, he told me that I needed to learn how to submit. I became highly offended, because I believed that being submitted meant giving and not receiving, unhappiness, control, domination, and loss of self-identity.

There it was that nasty "s" word. No one was going to tell me what I needed to do except my parents. I was so furious that I wanted to smack him. "What are you talking about?" I barked at him with my face all twisted up. "You can't tell me that I need to submit.

Number one, I am not even married to you yet. Number two, I went on, you don't tell a person that. I am not a dog. You don't tell me what to do and then I run and do it. Submission has to come from my heart; it's not something for you to tell me to do." He really missed it at that point because his attitude was all wrong. Telling me that I needed to submit was not going to cause me to do it.

It didn't matter how much scripture he showed me, told me, or I read. Even though I sensed that there was some truth in what he was saying, my perception of submission was so carnal, I wasn't going to do something that I felt had consequences that benefited him and not me. I had to pray because I knew that the spirit of God was already beginning to minister to me, but I needed a revelation on this submission thing, so that I could do what pleased God.

Submission and Humility – Products of A Willing Heart

God wants a willing heart. He wants a heart that wants to do things His way. One way that this is achieved is through humility (the act of putting aside any haughtiness, lofty thinking, arrogance, or know-it-all mentalities). Looking at God's building model, Exodus 35, you can see that God wasn't interested in receiving from a heart that gave grudgingly, resentfully or even out of obligation. Before the Israelites could submit to the plan of God, they had to first humble themselves. God wanted people who carefully followed directions (obedient) with an attitude of submission and humility.

He wanted people who knew that they couldn't possibly do such an awesome task without divine direction. He didn't want people who put their "personal touch" on his creation. The Bible says that God is opposed to the proud, but he gives grace to the humble (James 4:6). In essence, when we begin to believe that we need God's Word and wisdom, he will give us grace (supernatural favor) to focus so that we can submit to our husbands as "unto the Lord".

After humility has been established, submission must be displayed. Some of the Israelites wouldn't humble themselves. Moses told all of the children of Israel what God needed for them to do in order to build the temple. Each Israelite had an opportunity to let God's word minister to them so that they could prepare their hearts for the service of building. God gave them the chance to humble themselves and submit. But not all of them chose to, because some focused on the man, Moses, and not God. Some of the Israelites must have had a problem with submission, because "as many as" doesn't indicate that all of them were willing.

Exodus 35:22 says, "They came both men and women, **as many as** had a willing heart, and brought ..."

The principle of God's plan has not changed. He still wants willing hearted wives in which He can stir up and motivate to build their homes according to his plan. He is still looking for the meek, those who aren't so full of themselves that He can teach them the way He wants it done. He still looks for those who know that they can't build their households without Him. He is always ready to receive the offering of a willing heart.

Submission emerges from the heart of a wife who has humbled herself before God. She has decided to let His word renew her mind as she forsakes the carnal knowledge. Then, God's order of things becomes primary and her agenda secondary. But because society has taught women not to submit to anyone or anything, many of us have carried that carnal mentality into the kingdom of God and tried to function this way.

As a result of a lack of revelation and renewal of our minds to the Word on this subject, many wives refuse to submit to their own husbands. When they look at them, they see flaws, weaknesses, inadequacies. They see a husband who doesn't deserve to be the head of the household. Then, they begin to resent his position in the marriage, not realizing that they are in rebellion against God and his designated household order.

I once was that woman. I felt like my husband didn't deserve to be the head of our household sometimes. I became angry with God and wondered why in the world he made my husband the head. Why did I have to be accountable to him? There were things that I knew to be right regardless of what he thought or intended to inter-ject. But God answered me plain and simple, when you rebel against him, you rebel against me. You are out of order.

Submission is like an artery through which the grace of God flows

God designed our bodies to have blood circulating throughout it. He created the arterial system, a highly organized and intricately designed network of arteries within each of us to carry out this blood distribution assignment. Arteries are the main corridors through which blood is distributed from the heart to the vital tissues and organs of the body. Yet there are many factors that can contribute to the improper function of the arteries. Poor blood circulation, loss of blood circulation, and its complications is a major cause of death in the United States.

Arteriosclerosis is a condition where over a period of time, the arteries thicken and eventually harden as a result of ingesting sugary and fatty foods, starch ridden foods, cigarettes, alcohol, or cholesterol laden delicacies over a period of time. These fatty substances cling to the walls of the arteries restricting the flow of blood to vital organs and tissues. As a result, the blood doesn't flow as God intended for it to and the whole body suffers. A change in eating habits (diet), regular exercise, quitting cigarettes and abandoning alcohol, may help to prevent this process early in life.

Submission, like the arterial system, is the divinely designed system of order through which God flows his grace to every vital area of a person's life. That grace (favor) is sufficient to meet each emotional, physical, relationship-oriented, mental, financial, career, or ministry need, you will ever have. 2 Corinthians 12:9 tells us that God's grace is sufficient for us and that his power is perfected in our weakness. Although the grace of God is unmerited, we can position ourselves to receive it all of the time.

However, some women in the body of Christ today don't have God's grace flowing on a consistent basis. They are out of order. Their arteries are clogged with fatty, self-serving things like: bitterness, carnal attitudes, rebellion, haughtiness, ungodly counsel, unforgiveness, and misconceptions about the truth of God's Word, so that His grace is stifled.

When a Believer is out of God's order, she can't receive the benefit of regularly accessing his grace. As a result, worry, stress, and fear have the potential to dominate her life. However, if godly principles are exercised, carnal habits are neglected, and a steady diet of word application is applied, then the fatty deposits can be washed out by the Word and there will be nothing there to restrict God's grace from freely flowing.

After being married for a couple of months, the Lord made it obvious to me that I had fatty substances (fleshly issues) that hindered the flow of His grace in my life. I had so many misconceptions about what submission was and what it was not. My flesh rebelled against the very idea of it in some areas of my married life. I figured that my husband didn't esteem my voice in a matter, because he would do what he wanted to do anyway. Yet, this was far from the truth. My husband rarely did anything without talking to me about it first and asking for my input - but that wasn't enough for me at the time. On the inside, I wanted my will or what I believed God told me to supersede whatever he had to offer.

I thought that submitting to my husband was not much more than obedience, or fulfilling some of his requests. My perception of submission was all wrong. Carnal thinking taught me that as long as I had dinner on the table, kept the house clean and in order, run some errands for him, and wash the clothes, I was being submitted. After I filled those obligations, I felt that I should be able to make household decisions independent of him and I was entitled to have whatever I wanted.

As the Holy Spirit continued to minister to me in this area, I searched the Word, and my deliverance came as a result of 4 short words in Ephesians 5:22 - AS UNTO THE LORD. Submission wasn't solely about serving my husband and him serving me. It wasn't about him controlling me or not esteeming me properly. But, it was about understanding his God appointed position and role and my God appointed position and role in our household as it relates to the kingdom of God. As I meditated this further, the Lord began to share some significant points with me.

10 Things to Remember about Obedience,
Submission and God's Grace

1. Obedience is easy; it is merely doing what is asked.
2. Submission requires you to humble yourself to the will and order of God.

3. God ordained your husband to be the head of your house; You must let him be that.
4. Submitting means that you have to accept the fact that your husband is the head of your marriage, then esteem his position with your attitude and actions.
5. Once you allow God to show you how to be a proper helpmeet, then you will be fulfilled.
6. It is your responsibility to share with your husband or bring to his attention the wisdom, insight or information that you gleaned from the Lord and his Word concerning any issues that pertained to both of you.
7. As you submit to your husband, he will submit to you.
8. You must have faith in God's word; therefore you have to speak God's promises to yourself concerning submission and humility.
9. As you submit, the Lord will give you favor (His grace will cover you) - He will speak to your husband
10. He will direct your husband's decisions, and he won't let him make a decision that is outside of his good, acceptable or perfect will.

Even though I knew that this could be a little difficult for me, I chose to believe the Word of God. His grace was sufficient for me and his power was perfected in my weakness. I needed his grace to submit, even though it was AS UNTO THE LORD.

I needed his power to overcome the carnal thoughts about submission that popped up in my mind. But in order for me to have the grace, I had to do something first - I had to act. I had to make a faith move. I chose to believe that God heard me, if I humbled myself, whether my husband chose to or not. Then, I had to function as the wife God wanted me to be - void of all haughtiness, contention, and silent rebellion.

Psalm 10:17

> *LORD, thou hast heard the desire of the humble:*
> *thou wilt prepare their heart, thou wilt cause thine*
> *ear to hear:*

I no longer felt as if I had to have the only answer concerning many things, I continued to pray and give input, while trusting that God would give my husband the wisdom to make the right final decisions. Once I did this, I felt a tremendous burden lifted off of my shoulders. The Bible says that God's yoke is easy and his burden is light. Well, the burden of household accountability (headship) that I was carrying was so massive that just to get it to the feet of Jesus was a laborious task. That burden was heavy because God didn't authorize me to carry it.

God wants to take the unauthorized burdens out of your way, through the principle of submission, so that his grace can be administered to you. . James 4:7 says, "Therefore submit to God. Resist the devil and he will flee from you." Once I made the decision to submit to my husband AS UNTO THE LORD, carnal thoughts could no longer influence me to believe that submission was a horrible thing.

I began to practice this biblical principle as a way of life, and I have seen time and time again the grace of God kick in. I traded nagging my husband for casting my cares upon the Lord. I have watched the Lord give him wisdom in difficult situations and accelerate his decision making process. As I practiced this principle, God would impress upon him to apologize for not receiving my counsel. But, I practiced humility, not haughtiness ("I told you so" attitude) and God has blessed me.

Submission, if applied, will change your life forever. It is a fundamental life-changing principle that requires intense determination to humble oneself to God and then to express a part of that humility as submission to your husband. If you will follow this plan for your life, you will not hinder God's manifestation of grace in your life.

I now have a marriage in which there is only one agenda: God's agenda. My husband and I are jointly submitted to the plan and will of God for our marriage and family life, such that both of us receive his counsel regardless of the vessel through which it travels. My husband listens to me, asks for my counsel, esteems my counsel, and prayerfully considers it. Most of the time what I have shared with him is aligned to what God has already revealed to him for us.

Our household functions in godly order!

1 Corinthians 14:33
>*For God is not the author of confusion, but of peace, as in all churches of the saints.*

Skill #4 - Diligence

Proverbs 12:27b NASB
>*But the precious possession of a man is diligence.*

Diligence: Your life is as Leaven: Cake Mix

Most cakes consist of the same basic ingredients like sugar, eggs, oil or butter, and a leavening ingredient. The leaven may be in the form of yeast, baking soda, baking powder or even a can of pop. Ultimately, this ingredient reacts with the sugar and other ingredients in the mixture to produce carbon dioxide. And it is by the release of the carbon dioxide that the cake will rise. It's like blowing air into the mixture from the inside out. No matter what form it comes in, the leaven is only beneficial when it reacts with the mixture and produces the carbon dioxide.

The interesting thing about leaven is that there is no substitute for it. If a recipe calls for it, and you neglect to add it, the mixture will not rise and the cake will be flat. Even if you started out with the freshest of ingredients and the best bake ware, without leaven the cake will not look or taste like you intended it to. Your expectations will have been unmet.

Diligence is like that leaven. There is no substitute for it. Diligence is the faithful, disciplined and consistent application of God's Word in our lives. That means that we esteem the Word enough to do it on a regular basis, even if it takes us out of our comfort zone at times. We can't haphazardly approach the Word and expect to receive the benefits illustrated therein. We can't occasionally humble ourselves, seldom submit, or periodically fear the Lord and expect for the Word of God to consistently net the promises written.

Like unleavened cake, a believer's life void of any diligence will lack the quality and consistency necessary to be a witness and a testimony to a world that needs to see and come to Jesus. We must make the decision to regularly and consistently walk in his uncompromising Word with the expectation of seeing the results the word illustrates. There are many areas where we are commanded to be diligent. However, here are 2 areas that changed my life and caused me to begin building my house, instead of tearing it down: diligence over my heart and diligence in resting

Diligence over your heart

Proverbs 4:23-27
> *Watch over your heart with all diligence, for from it flow the springs of life. Put away from you a deceitful mouth, And put devious lips far from you. Let your eyes look directly ahead, And let your gaze be fixed straight in front of you. Watch the path of your feet, And all your ways will be established. Do not turn to the right nor to the left; Turn your foot from evil.*

Early in my marriage, I believed that Proverbs 4:23 meant that I was supposed to be careful about who I was to get close to, so that I wouldn't get hurt or let down. I thought that if I didn't watch over and guard my heart that I would be in for a lot of disappointing times or maybe even get a broken heart. Yet as I meditated this scripture, God showed me that my heart was home to some biblical principles and it was home to a mind heavily influenced by the world.

For on my heart the Word was written and out of it's abundance I spoke. My heart was to be a sanctuary for the Holy Word of God. I couldn't function with an unrenewed, carnal, worldly mind and expect the bountiful marriage that I hoped and believed for. Therefore, I couldn't allow those things that were ungodly to come into my heart and dwell with those things that were of Him. I had to diligently work at changing the composition of my heart, by renewing my mind to the Word of God. In other words, I had to intently watch over and screen the things that I saw and heard before I did three things:

- entertained them in my mind
- allowed them to influence my will
- let them steer my emotions.

In the beginning of our marriage, my husband did some things that I considered to be quite annoying and immature. On many occasions I felt as if I were his mother. This feeling intensified as I heard stories from other Believers about their husbands acting like little boys or big babies. In my heart and with my mouth, I agreed with them. My heart became so abundant with the notion that most husbands acted like big kids at one time or another that I began to speak it with my mouth, then to my husband. I let him know that I wasn't going to be his mother.

Monthly, I read through the book of Proverbs and each time I came to chapter 4, God spoke to me about my increasing frustration with feeling like I was my husband's momma. Though I felt frustrated, I never looked at the Word to see what God said about my husband. I just agreed with what the world said about men: they're like big kids. The more I agreed with this, the more frustrated with him I became. I couldn't let it happen anymore. My peace was dwindling.

However, as the Lord began to deal with me concerning Proverbs 4:23, I began to actively watch over my heart. I raised my spiritual antennas and I became very aware of whatever tried to enter my heart. I rejected anything that didn't line up with the Word of God. I learned to cherish it as a place where the Word dwelled, and I wanted to be a good steward over it. It seemed like as soon as I made that decision, the Lord gave me an opportunity to practice watching over my heart.

One day while leaving our Sunday morning services, a visitor stopped to tell me how blessed she was by the message my husband had given. Then she said, "Oh you have your hands full with three kids!" and I said, "Three? I only have two children" then she nudged me and giggled, "Your other child, get it? You know how those men are, they're just like children." At that point, I became pretty intent not to let those comments enter into my heart, so I calmly said, "No my husband is not like a child, and I don't mind having 2 kids close in age." After that, she changed the subject and eventually left. Later, when she visited our church again, she made a similar comment. This time, I took a few minutes to share with her how God dealt with me about diligently watching over my heart. She understood and received it well.

Her ignorant comments were indicative of the world's perception of men or husbands. If I neglected to stand guard over my heart, and would have allowed it to enter in, as I had in the past, I would have done several things. First, I would have believed and confessed the lie that my husband was like a little child. Second, I would have continued being frustrated with him for acting like a child, when I wanted a man.

Third, I would have received her comments into my heart, and eventually treated him like a child. Fourth, I would have put myself in the position to disobey the Word of God in Ephesians. Ephesians 5:33 told me to make sure that I respected my husband and Ephesians 5:22 said that he was the head of our household. I couldn't properly respect him as a man of God, if in my heart I saw him as and treated him like a child.

The truth about my husband was that he was head of our household, just as Christ is the head of the church. The grown man Jesus didn't act like a little child. No matter how my husband may have acted at different times, the Lord's description of him wasn't that of a child.

As I consistently filled my heart up and meditated what the word of God said concerning him, I was able to detect the lie and reject it. I worked hard at recognizing and discerning those things that weren't supposed to enter. I also worked hard at making the Word of God preeminent in my heart, so that I spoke it with my mouth.

This incident was a critical turning point for me. When I realized that I had to take information that I had seen or heard and consistently reject it if it didn't line up with God's Word (especially in the area of marriage) I began to renew my mind to His Word. The composition of my heart began to change. The truth of God's word became predominant in my heart and it influenced what I thought about him, what I desired from him, and how I felt with him.

Romans 12:2

> *And be not conformed to this world: but be ye trans-*
> *formed by the renewing of your mind, that ye may*
> *prove what is that good, and acceptable, and*
> *perfect, will of God.*

Wisdom: My Supernatural Security Force

Many superstars hire well-trained bodyguards who by nature of their appearance often intimidate would be attackers or protect them from other dangerous situations. But, no matter how menacing the bodyguard may look, no matter how well their senses are trained, it's their ability to consistently be alert, diligent, and on guard that will protect a client. These costly bodyguards are trained to see what the superstar doesn't see, hear or sense. As they protect, they stay close to their client and monitor their personal space.

God considers the human heart to be a precious possession worthy to be protected by the most powerful supernatural security force available. Your heart has the capacity to contain valuable treasure and must be shielded from invasions of destructive things that come to seize a place in the believer's heart like: bitterness, resentment, rebellion, unforgiveness, anger, hatred, jealousy, and fear.

The heart is the center of all physical and spiritual life. A Believer's heart houses the soul (mind, will, emotions, imaginations and intellectual capacity) and the regenerated spirit (the God empowered governor over your soul). Your heart is a powerful entity that has the capacity to do God's will and to disobey God's Word:

Do God's Will

Hide the Word	Psalm 119:11
Have faith	Hebrews 10:22
Possess a meek spirit	1 Peter 3:4
Do the will of God	Ephesians 6:6
Stand steadfast	1 Corinthians 7:37
Believe	Romans 10:9-10
Meditate	Psalm 49:3
Speak	Psalm 53:1

Disobey God's Will

Be Stubborn	Jeremiah 18:12
Condemn yourself	1 John 3:20
Deceive yourself	James 1:26
Err (go astray)	Hebrews 3:10
Sin	Matthew 5:28
War	Psalm 55:21

A heart that receives and hides God's Word in it is worthy of protection, it must be guarded. Wisdom, diligently applied, is like the supernatural security force that has the capability to guard your heart.

Ecclesiastes 7:12
> *For wisdom is a defence, and money is a defence:*
> *but the excellency of knowledge is, that wisdom*
> *giveth life to them that have it.*

Wisdom is a defense. Wisdom defends, protects and guards our hearts. Best of all, this supernatural security is free. The Word teaches us in James 1:5 that if we ask for wisdom, God will give it to us freely. His wisdom will cause us to see, hear and sense what we couldn't before, while showing us ways to handle situations.

Like the bodyguard, if we allow it to, God's word can stay close and escort us to every event we attend, every dinner we eat, every meeting we go to, and every phone call we make. It can even assist us with every decision we make or counsel we give. But we must choose to employ it. A bodyguard can't protect his client if she won't allow him to be with her. Wisdom can't protect or defend if it's not used.

But when harmful things that come to seize a place in our hearts, (i.e.: gossip calls, unforgiveness develops, offenses taunt, or lusts provoke), we can speak the Word to take these offenders into captivity. When we speak the Word of God in the midst of these attacks, we are releasing the Supernatural security force out to take care of business. As a result, godly wisdom apprehends the attackers, renders them swift judgment, and prevents these things from invading your heart. God has given us charge over our own hearts. All we have to do is consistently heed the Word, hear the Word, do the Word, and speak the Word. His supernatural security will do the rest.

Diligence in Resting

Psalms 71:3

> *Be thou my strong habitation, whereunto I may continually resort: thou hast given commandment to save me; for thou art my rock and my fortress.*

Have you ever been told that you needed to take a vacation? Maybe even go to some luxurious spa and resort type place where you could rest and relax. Most of us don't have to think twice about it. We would be on our way in an instant if we could put the trip in the hands of someone else to plan and pay for. Yet many of us don't have that option. We must do the work to prepare for a vacation. We must count the cost away from work, the financial responsibilities to make it worthwhile, etc... Then we make the choice: Is this vacation that I've planned worth the time and money?

Be Thou My Strong Habitation, whereunto I may continually resort.......

This was my scenario concerning our marriage many years ago. To me, our honeymoon was like a vacation. It was a place where we prayed, had good discussions, made decisions, and genuinely enjoyed one another. But once our honeymoon was over and our newlywed issues began to surface, my picture of long lasting marital tranquility and peace seemed like a fantasy. I wasn't married a good 3 months and I needed a break. My picture of our lifelong vacation was blurred by arguments, communication difficulties, and general differences in our upbringing. I needed a rest, a vacation. I wanted to resort somewhere away from "him".

I didn't want to be separated or divorced. I just wanted to get away every now and then to rest from the arguments, frustrations, and feelings of inadequacy. Yet in my heart, I wanted to be the ultimate wife, who went above and beyond and was cherished by her husband. But I felt as if I couldn't develop or express this part of myself because in my view, he had some issues that he needed to work out – and they were *his* issues – not mine.

I felt desperate and little confused. Who was I to this man God placed me with? Was I a housewife? A mother? A child bearer? A maid? A cook? A teacher? A servant? A professional? A minister? A student? An administrator? An over comer? I wasn't so opinionated any more. I just wanted our marriage to work the way that God said that it would. At this point, I relied upon God to be my strong habitation. I went to him in prayer over and over and over again. Even though I didn't watch a lot of TV, I turned the TV off. I spent time with the Lord in prayer and fasting. HE became my resort. I didn't physically need to go anywhere. I just needed to focus on hearing from God, obey what HE told me to do and then rest in HIM until he brought what I believed for in our marriage.

Matthew 11:29-30

> *Take My yoke upon you and learn from Me, for I am gentle and humble in heart; and YOU SHALL FIND REST FOR YOUR SOULS. For my yoke is easy and my burden is light.*

God wanted me to rest in HIM. My soul needed a vacation. It was wearing me out.

- My unrenewed mind kept telling me to do what I felt like doing. It kept reminding me of what the world told me about my husband (they're immature little kids).
- I continued to entertain thoughts that told me I wasn't appreciated and that I wasted my time getting a degree because I wouldn't use it sitting at home as a "housewife".
- I had to keep casting down imaginations of what life would be like if minimal marital growth took place. What if I was stuck? What if he stayed like this forever? Would I ever be truly happy?

My soul (unrenewed part of me) was wearing me out because it kept contending with God's written Word (Jer. 29:11) and the Word that I knew God spoke to me a year earlier. Before my husband and I married, a man of God spoke a prophetic word over us. In that Word, God told us that our marriage would be like a satellite and that marriages all over would be touched, affected and changed by the ministry that we were to have.

I had to stop compromising with my unrenewed mind and put on the mind of Christ. I had to see my marriage the way that HE intended for it to be. So, as I continued to pursue God's will for my life through the Word, I began to see something special. I began to see who God said that I was and my importance in the kingdom. I had a career path that was ordained from the foundations of the world. Having gotten married 3 months out of college, my first marital assignment along that path was that of a builder. It was my responsibility to make sure that I built my house. It didn't matter how the world viewed "stay at home moms" or "housewives".

Sure, I stayed at home, but that wasn't who I was. I wasn't a housewife. I was a help meet who had to make sure that I didn't hinder the growth of our household. Did I begin building it with natural materials? No. I had to use principles from the Word of God as the chief cornerstone and from there everything was to line up with him and the Word.

Hebrews 4:10-12

> *For he that is entered into his rest, he also hath ceased from his own works, as God did from his.*
> *Let us labour therefore to enter into that rest, lest any man fall after the same example of unbelief.*
>
> *For the word of God is quick, and powerful, and sharper than any two edged sword, piercing even to the dividing asunder of soul and spirit, and of the joints and marrow, and is a discerner of the thoughts and intents of the heart.*

God wanted my soul to rest from its constant churning of the world's way of thinking and doing things. He wanted me to have the ultimate vacation that would last a lifetime. On that vacation, I would do some work - but if I learned from Him, his yoke was easy and his burden was light.

My vacation was already planned. Your vacation has already been planned. All I had to do was to agree to take it. God promised me rest. In verse 11 he told me to be diligent to enter that rest, so that I wouldn't fall because of disobedience. The Bible clearly told me that if I was disobedient or in unbelief, I couldn't enter into his rest.

The Greek word for rest is Anapausis, which means to pause from labor. God wanted me to take a break, to pause from operating under the mindset that was not renewed by His word and then to pick up his yoke and with vigor begin resting in Him and his promises. Resting is no lazy or idle task. When we rest in the promises of God, we have got to get a hold of them, receive them into our hearts, speak them with our mouths, obey his Word and be relentless in our belief that God will bring them to pass.

I had already been disobedient and restless. Now, I had to obey God even when HE told me to do things that I didn't want to do. I had to stop doubtfully looking at the circumstances and begin to believe that I could have the life that God showed me in his Word. I had to believe that I would be valuable in my home and be as highly honored as the woman in Proverbs 31:10-31.

I have seen and continue to see the rewards of resting my soul and working His word in my life through speaking and believing it. As I work diligently to stay rested in the promises of God, and active in confessing God's word with my mouth, my faith continues to increase. It is no longer a challenge to believe that God is going to do what he said he would do in my life.

I am living in the reality of the blessings of obedience (to building my household) even now. It didn't take over a decade to receive them either. God has and is prospering our lives, marriage, children, family life, finances and much much more. In 12 years, here are just a few of the things that we have experienced as a result of my focusing on building the household as the helpmeet God designed for me to be:

- A joyful marriage that becomes more and more fulfill-

ing each year
- Our Children increasingly blessed in their relationship w/the Lord, school work and favor
- Blessed and prosperous ministry reaching across the nation w/thousands of lives changed
- Favor with those in authority
- Financial increase of our household salary 10 times that of when we first married

Here are some of the promises in God's word that I confessed and believed for God to manifest in my life. Below each scripture is a revelation truth that I grasped from the scripture:

Proverbs 10:4
Poor is he who works with a negligent hand, but the hand of the diligent makes rich.

- God will make me rich, so I can be a blessing, if I diligently and relentlessly walk in the principles illustrated in His word.

Proverbs 13:4
The soul of the sluggard craves and gets nothing, but the soul of the diligent is made fat.

- God will prosper and anoint my mind, will, emotions, imagination and intellect, if I don't neglect His plan.

Proverbs 21:5
The plans of the diligent lead surely to advantage, but everyone who is hasty comes surely to poverty.

- God will abundantly manifest His purpose in me, if I make my soul rest in Him.

Skill # 5 - Respect

Ephesians 5:33 (Amplified Bible)
> *However, let each man of you [without exception]*
> *love his wife as [being in a sense] his very own self;*
> *and let the wife see that she respects and reverences*
> *her husband [that she notices him, regards him,*
> *honors him, prefers him, venerates, and esteems*
> *him; and that she defers to him, praises him, and*
> *loves and admires him exceedingly].*

Over the years, I have had the blessed opportunity to counsel many married women. Most of them have found it difficult to respect their husbands. No matter how long they've been married, most didn't know that to respect their spouse was not a suggestion, but a command. It is a commandment from God's word that women ignore either on accident or by choice. Many feel that if love is there, respect is there too. However that is not always the case.

Before my mind was renewed to the Word in this area, though saved, I believed with a carnal mentality. I felt that my husband was not worthy of my respect until he knocked me off of my feet with a thoughtful gift or permanent change of attitude. I treated him nicely, but respect was a big thing to me. It meant I looked up to him. He didn't need that, I rationalized. He is too macho. He needs to come off of his high horse a little bit, stop acting like he has everything in control and act like he really needs me, not just wants me - I thought.

Contrary to the way that he sometimes talked to me, his occasional flare-ups, and his inability to promptly handle some of our marital problems in our first several months together, I knew deep down inside of my heart and in my spirit that he loved me. He really loved me. No matter how mad we would each get, he would always end our conversation with I love you and a hug. Whenever he came home from work, no matter what type of attitude either one of us had, he would say I love you and give me a firm, yet gentle hug. He did it so much, that I often told him to stop it.

The Respect Question

One day, while on his way upstairs to change clothes, my husband asked me a question that took me by surprise. "Do you respect me?" he belted out. Where did that come from? I thought. Then I began to get a little indignant, "What do you mean respect you?" I said somewhat puzzled. "I mean, do you respect me?" he said as if irritated to repeat the question. I thought about it for another second because something about that question bothered me and then I said, "Well I don't know what you mean by that. I know what the word respect means, but I don't know if I respect you or not. Based on my concept of respect - I guess not."

I thought he meant respect in the sense of being in awe of or reverencing him - like I worshipped God. So I figured there is no way in the world that I would respect him, not like that. Then the Lord began to deal with me from Ephesians 5:33.

To put things into their proper perspective, the Lord shared a couple of things with me about the respect that I ought to have for my husband. First, He reminded me of the fact that Ben was his child and that I was to respect him as a man of God, unto Him — just like the principle of submission. Second, I prayed that the Lord would show my husband to me through His eyes. Once he did this, I began to immediately see several reasons to respect him. I should respect him because of his:

- Relationship with God
- Faithfulness toward the things of God
- Uncompromising walk with the Lord
- Obedience toward God
- Integrity walk
- Love that he consistently expressed for me

Then he told me that the world's concept of a good marriage was irrelevant to me. My marriage was to be based on godly principles and couldn't be compared to an unbeliever's marriage. I then began to realize that a Christian woman should concentrate on building her marriage with the components of submission and respect. Both of which are done "AS UNTO THE LORD".

I had a lot of work to do. But when I began to act upon these things, I experienced an immediate difference in his whole attitude and my own! As you read, and meditate these things for yourself, be relentless. Don't give up until you are able to fulfill these expressions of respect.

Ephesians 5:33 (Amplified)

> *However, let each man of you [without exception] love his wife as [being in a sense] his very own self; and let the wife see that she respects and reverences her husband [that she notices him, regards him, honors him, prefers him, venerates and esteems him; and that she defers to him, praises him, and loves and admires him exceedingly].*

Notice Him (become aware of him)

I began to notice him when we were out in public or when he would minister and I would look at him and find things to admire about him: how he wore his clothes, the way that he talked, and his boldness and confidence in who he was in Christ. I began to look at his strengths, which were areas that I was often weak in - and he became my built-in spiritual role model. Although he wasn't perfect, there were some things that I needed to learn from him and once I learned to respect him, I was willing to receive from him. Now that I honored him and looked up to him, he was more apt to receive from me as well.

Regard Him (to see him as possessing specific qualities)

The more that I took notice of him, the more that I recognized some of his qualities as things that I needed to re-adapt into my own lifestyle. My husband led a spiritually disciplined lifestyle. He fasted weekly, he studied and meditated his word daily and he did his daily devotions before going to work every morning. On the other hand, I fasted periodically and didn't study daily. Watching him walk in that disciplined lifestyle and seeing the supernatural results caused me to study more and fast more often.

Honor Him (to esteem him based upon virtue)

He walked in integrity like no one I had ever seen. He was a man of his word. He prayerfully accepted responsibilities, so that he wouldn't become over burdened with them and have to turn some of them down. This was so important to me, and I honored him for that. Because of his integrity, I counted him dependable. I knew that when he said he would do something or be somewhere that he would be true to his word. I felt as if I wouldn't be let down, by empty promises, as I was in past relationships. I honored him for that.

Prefer Him (to like him above all)

I also began to prefer him. I stopped making mental comparisons concerning his appearance, attitude, conversation, or anything with past beaus. I also ceased to expect him to respond to me the way others did. Instead, I focused on the man God gave to me. I began to notice how unique and special he was. I looked for those attributes in him that I wouldn't trade for anything. The things that he had to offer were things that I needed. He became special in my eyes for the first time and I realized what God had truly blessed me with.

Venerate & Esteem Him (develop a high opinion of him)

Despite the immaturity that he may have displayed in his character periodically, I made the decision not to consider my husband as a little child or a big baby. Then, I began to appraise him based upon God's standard. God saw him as His son, who was worthy of his inheritance. His word said that he was the head of our household and a mighty man of valor and that was how I decided to see him.

Defer to Him (to consider and value his judgment and allow it to weigh more heavily than your own)

Once I began to see my husband as the head of our household, I began to value his judgment more greatly than before. Both of us valued the Word above our petty issues, so we agreed that we wouldn't face each other with opinions or fleshly desires, but with the Word. However if the Lord hadn't spoken to him specifically about something or our situation he would suggest a plan of action. He'd start out by saying, "I would prefer if you did this, or, it would be better if you did that."

So when I needed to make a decision on something, I felt comfortable asking him what he thought about it. Often what he said would settle in my spirit and I would do what he suggested. However, when I felt as though I had a definitive answer from the Lord and he didn't, then I would tell him what I believe God told me and it would usually settle peacefully in his spirit or we would pray about it some more.

I was not a passive person, but I feared God. I knew by then, that I was protected by and showered with the grace of God when I submitted to the head that God placed in my life. I also knew that submission was not just obedience, but valuing my husband's judgment enough to follow through with it, since I believed that he had my best interests at heart. He wouldn't suggest for me to do anything because he wanted to control me. He almost always gave me suggestions that lined up with the Word of God - and I *refused* to reject them.

Praise Him (to speak with approval of him)

I couldn't just sit by on the sidelines and let him do phenomenal things and not compliment or comment anymore. On the inside, I would be proud of him and blessed to be his wife, but I didn't tell him that. I had to decide to support him with my mouth. When he would finish ministering or counseling someone, I would tell him how much of blessing it was and how he really let the Lord use him. I would tell him that he chose good analogies and examples and that they really helped everyone to capture the essence of the scriptural principles that he was teaching. I had to tell him that I *liked* him. I had to tell him that I enjoyed being his wife. He appreciated it so much that he did wonderful things for me!

Love & Admire Him (begin to contemplate him with pleasure)

When I thought about my husband, I had to choose to contemplate him with pleasure. I had to enjoy thinking about him and how he blessed me. I had to put aside all of the minor eccentricities that I once focused on, so that I could have something to cherish about him. So what if he didn't know how to do some of the household things that my father knew how to do. He still blessed me in many ways and made sure that I didn't lack anything.

Once I learned to truly respect my husband in all of these different ways, I became a fulfilled wife who was married to a fulfilled husband!

Skill # 6 & 7 – Love & Faith

1 Corinthians 13:4-8 (in part)
> *Charity suffereth long, and is kind; charity envieth not; charity vaunteth not itself, is not puffed up, Doth not behave itself unseemly, seeketh not her own, is not easily provoked, thinketh no evil; Rejoiceth not in iniquity, but rejoiceth in the truth; Beareth all things, believeth all things, hopeth all things, endureth all things. Charity never faileth . . .*

Some of us are familiar with the biblical definition of love in 1 Corinthians 13. Yet few of us ever walk in love to this degree. Our perception of love has been shaped by our emotions, our surroundings and the fulfillment of selfish desires. We love someone when they have pleased us. We love something when it has met our highest standards. We love someone when they do what we want them to do. In essence, we have reduced love to a warm and fuzzy selfish feeling that we get when we favor, approve, or lust over someone or something. The world's method of love will not assist a woman of God in building her home, but it will like a wrecking tool bring destruction.

Ephesians 5:2 NASB
> *And walk in love, just as Christ also loved you, and gave Himself up for us, an offering and a sacrifice to God as a fragrant aroma.*

Love is essential in keeping a household in true spiritual harmony. God commands the Believer in Ephesians 5:2 to "walk in love" or "live a life of love", yet we often misunderstand what He is really saying here. Loving those who are loveable is easy, but to love those spouses, brothers and sisters who disappoint, provoke or offend us often presents a challenge.

Some believers have confused the love walk with a heroic feat of strength when they pat themselves on the back for speaking to or hugging someone who they "don't get along with". Others have confused love with a strained sugary sweet demonstration of tolerance toward someone that has "offended" them. Yet others feel that if they just say the words, "Love you sister or Love you brother" that the requirement to walk in love is being met. But these acts alone are not indicative of a person who walks in love.

Walking is the way we travel. In order to get from destination A to destination B, whether we fly, drive or sail, at one point or another we must walk. Our legs and feet don't just pick up and start moving. When we want to walk to the mailbox, we make the decision to do it and then our bodies and everything in them works together to follow suit.

The Greek word for walk (in Eph. 5:2) is peripateo, to walk at large. "At large" has numerous meanings, but the most compelling definition that God presented to me for walking at large is this: The Believer's love walk is to be represented by the whole body, not just a part of it. Walking in love is the way that the Believer goes from point A to point B, from faith to faith, and from glory to glory. The Bible says that faith works by love (Gal. 5:6). If we don't walk in love, our faith can not move, it can't grow, and we can not please God.

So why is it so difficult to walk in love sometimes? Well, simply put, it takes work. The Greek word Peripateo (walk) also means to freely trample a path. When a path is first being made, it is like conquering new ground. A land developer doesn't just go into a wooded area and voila there is a path. He must get his construction crew to knock down trees, kill the shrubs, and till the ground. What once existed there has to be destroyed and replaced with alternate materials. Then, he can see a path to walk on.

As a Believer, redeemed by the blood of Jesus, we are free to love. We are no longer bound by false sense of love (counterfeit love) as the world is:

Proverbs 26:23 Amplified
*Burning lips [uttering insincere words of love] and a
wicked heart are like an earthen vessel covered with
the scum thrown off from molten silver [making it
appear to be solid silver].*

The Bible says that we have the ability to love, because Christ
loved us first. As we learn to walk in love, we will knock down our
past hurts, crucify our flesh, and till the new ground of our hearts in
preparation for a love walk that will last a lifetime.

So how do we love? How do we begin to attain the characteristics of love in 1 Corinthians 13? How do we have patience with our
husbands while they attempt something that we have given them
insight not to attempt? How do we not become provoked when a
sister or brother in the Lord who has always seemed to be a decent
person purposely pushes your hot button? God's answer to me in
the midst of these challenges was this:

1 Timothy 1:5 NASB
*But the goal of our instruction is to love from a pure
heart, a good conscience and a sincere faith.*

There are 3 parts of our being that must be renewed in order for
love to produce the offspring illustrated in 1 Corinthians: heart,
mind, will. All three of these things are a part of the soul.

A Pure Heart, A Good Conscience, A Sincere Faith
Biblical love is the product of the obedient, pure, and undefiled
heart. If you want to know what is in your heart, listen to what
comes out of your mouth.

Matthew 15:18, 19 NASB
*But the things that proceed out of the mouth come
from the heart, and those defile the man. For out of
the heart come evil thoughts, murders, adulteries,
fornications, thefts, false witness, slanders.*

In principle, the Word says that if we entertain (meditate and day dream about) sinful acts (actions against the will of God) - then we have committed those acts already in our own heart. These sinful acts are not just limited to what is in this scripture, but include such things as: rebellion against authority, revenge against someone who has offended us, and disobedience to the Word (doing what we want to do- when we know what the Word says to do).

About 5 or 6 years ago I was in a situation where I discovered that I wasn't walking in the love that God talks about in 1 Timothy 1:5. As I re-evaluated my thoughts and actions, the Lord dealt with me concerning my heart. I had a total spiritual make-over in my heart - and from this experience the Lord taught me how to walk in love with my husband, children, and brothers and sisters in the Lord.

Here's what happened:

There was a sister in the church who would offend me almost every time that I saw her. She would compliment me in one ear and slander me in the other. One moment she would tell me how much I was a blessing to her and the church. Not too long after that, she would literally get in my face and point and yell that I was of the devil and that I was going to hell.

Obviously, whenever I saw her, I tried to avoid her. However, this was difficult, because I had to work with her very closely in one of the ministries of our church. I wasn't fearful, but I felt like she was crazy and I had to be prepared to defend myself - physically when around her. I felt so uncomfortable around her that I told my husband about her comments and sporadic verbal assaults that she made toward me. He watched to make sure that I was not in danger and he often reminded me to keep her in prayer - so I did.

Though I prayed for her, I continued to verbally rehearse the offenses to my husband and then to my parents, who lived nearly 2000 miles away (as I asked for them to keep her and me in prayer). I also began to imagine myself doing things or saying things to hurt her. In other words, I meditated revengeful acts. I wouldn't call the sister names, but I questioned her walk with the Lord. How could someone who says that they love the Lord and hears from him, intentionally offend me and act so evil at times? How can I love someone who seems as if they find things to say in order to offend me?

I knew that I was supposed to walk in love, and I didn't want to be a hypocrite and say that I loved her when I really didn't. I knew that I didn't love her. So I began to speak to the sister instead of avoid her, while wearing a smile of uncertainty on my face. At this point, I thought that I was trying - but it didn't feel right. How in the world was I supposed to love this woman, who I dared to call my "sister"? So as I began to search the scriptures on love, the Lord spoke to me through 1Timothy 1:5. This scripture taught me how to love. It said that I had to love her with a pure heart, a good conscience, and a sincere faith. I wasn't even close!! So I began to check myself.

1. I didn't love her with a pure heart because my mouth continued to spew all of the offenses that took place. I didn't recall offending her, so I couldn't understand her blatant attempts to verbally tear me apart. So, my heart was hurt because I didn't feel that I deserved to be treated the way that she treated me. Little did I know that it was my presence that offended her. As a result, out of the abundance of my heart, my mouth spoke. I questioned her character, her relationship with the Lord, and her salvation.

2. I didn't love her with a good conscience, because I kept dwelling on her offensive behavior. I thought about it so much after seeing her, that I began to imagine myself in physical altercations with her, as I pondered how to physically subdue and hurt her. As a result, I sinned by meditating revengeful acts against her.

3. I didn't even love her with a sincere faith, because deep down inside, I had neither a shallow belief nor a strong conviction that this woman was going to allow the Lord to minister to her. I had seen her totally disrespect and rebel against her husband on several occasions -to the point of bringing him shame. By choice she did these things, so if she chose to do these things, why would she

choose to let the Lord deal with her- she hasn't yet - I reasoned with myself. Even though I prayed for her, my faith concerning her change wasn't sincere. I honestly didn't believe it would happen. My eyes weren't focused on what God could do, but on what she did. With this attitude, my prayer for her was in vain.

In essence, my response to the offense was no better than the offense itself. How could I love the Lord who I hadn't seen, but couldn't love my sister, who I saw and worked with on Sunday mornings - despite her offensive behavior. I wanted to change. I wanted to love her the right way - God's way. I went to the source of love - God himself - through his Word and found the way. I owed it to God - to be obedient to his word. I owed it to myself not to allow my heart to stay defiled. I owed it to my family not to harbor and house resentful feelings and a lack of peace, so that my house could be established in love and not bitterness or unforgiveness.

This situation affected my household because I couldn't effectively minister to my husband or children. My mind was so preoccupied with the "ungodliness" of this woman and how she intentionally "wronged" me, that I rehearsed the incidents in my mind over and over again. I would try to forget about it, but I wouldn't.

So I repented to God for my behavior. Then I told the Lord that I wanted my heart to be right - and undefiled. I had to stop talking about how she wronged me, no matter how I felt about it. I also had to nurture a good conscience about her. I stopped meditating "what if" self - defense situations and revengeful words toward her. I began to meditate upon her as a delivered and changed woman. It wasn't easy, but I had to continually re-direct my mind in this area. I had to think on those things that were lovely, pure, of good report concerning her (Philippians 4:8).

Lastly, I had to sincerely believe that the Lord was going to complete his work in her, despite what I saw. Once I made this decision and began to walk in it, I was free. I would see her and even deal with her in church and no matter what she said - I saw her as the Lord saw her - his child. When I hugged her, it was so sincere - not a mere formality - and I loved her with the love of the Lord.

I can honestly say that no matter what situation I come up against, I will not neglect God's love as the motivation for all that I do in his name. I can't afford to. I have done the work, trampled a path and I will walk in love. I know that this is the only way to travel; it is the only way that my faith will consistently work. As I continue to build our household for the glory of God, I must keep myself motivated daily by his love and not just know about it - but walk in it.

BREAD PUDDING BREAKTHROUGH
A Word from Elder Ben Gibert

It's been more than 10 years now, but I remember it like it was yesterday. I was coming home from another full day at work. I was an Engineering manager working in Flint, Michigan. I was focused on my home life as I drove home. "What do I need to do when I get home? Maybe get something to eat, wash some clothes, check the mail and quickly begin preparing for some presentations later on in the week," I thought.

It had been a while since my wife had given me "the ultimatum". I had been washing my own clothes, warming my own food (if I missed the dinner hour) and praying for change for a few weeks. The Lord had shown me quite a few things about myself. I knew that I was far from perfect, but I wasn't sure how much longer I could keep up the current pace. Charisse was being a wife to me, but only what she felt was explicitly required.

As I pulled into the driveway I said a quick prayer (as was my custom). *Lord help me to maintain control, communicate more clearly, be patient. Help me to be a priest in my home not a manager or an executive. And Lord help me to remember that no matter what happens—Satan is my enemy never my wife. You have promised us a great life together- I believe that we receive it, in Jesus Name.*

When I gathered my briefcase from the backseat and turned to go toward the house. I heard the squeaky screen door open.

Charisse was in the door way. Maybe she wants to remind me to fix the door or maybe something is broken and she couldn't reach me. I was sure it had to be something she needed from me—- she never met me at the door. As I got closer to the doorway she was excitedly beckoning me to come in to the house. "Come on, come on! I want you to see something."

As I got closer, I began to meditate. "Even if we can't afford it now—sound excited—speak faith—don't crush her creativity—let her dream—It's part of your job as the priest. When I got to the door she grabbed my arm and almost dragged me to the basement. I almost dropped my briefcase down the steps. She was determined to take me on a tour of the house. She seemed happy enough, but this kind of intensity had never led to good things in the past.

She took me through the unfinished rec room area and back into the dark dingy laundry area. I felt bad—I knew that she didn't like basements, but this was all we could afford. Maybe there was a leak. She stopped at the entry and said, "What do you see?" At this point I was totally confused. After a few futile guesses, she just told me what the critical observation was.

"Ben, I've got all of your clothes taken care of—and I've found another laundry service for your shirts. It's cheaper and on your way to work. It should be much better for you." I still wasn't sure what was going on—so I just said, "Thank you honey". I started to go back up the stairs and she raced ahead of me. I blurted a warning, "Slow down honey, you are 6 months pregnant you know." I've got more to show you, come on," she said.

We went upstairs to the kitchen and she showed me 3 pots on the stove. "Open them", she insisted. When I did, I saw something that I had not seen in a long time. It was spaghetti (the normal size that she liked) and another pot with the thin angel hair variety that I prefer right beside it. "I made both, she said. I know you like the thinner type so I just made a separate pot for you."

At this point I knew something had changed, but I was almost scared to comment. My lovely wife took me to several other rooms and lovingly showed me things that she had done for me—phone calls, straightening etc. The 15 minute tour ended up again in the kitchen. She opened the oven and pulled out a round dish with some sort of food in it that I didn't recognize. "I made this for you, I hope you like it."

Sheepishly I asked, "What is it?" "It's bread pudding. It is a Louisiana recipe. You said you really liked your mom's bread pudding. I couldn't reach her so I got this from a book and spiced it up a bit based on what you like. I think you'll like it." At this point I just hugged her and told her I loved her. I told her I was sorry for any of the mistakes I had made in our young marriage – and that I appreciated everything she had done and ever would do to make our home Godly and successful. I never asked her to apologize for any of the things that I thought were wrong or explain what had happened that changed her so much that day.

We just began to move forward. Every day, week, month and year since then has been a glorious growth experience. My wife has truly lived every principle in this book. I've seen her cry, push, grow and conquer sometimes all in a single week. Her devotion to doing things God's way is inspiring to me and has been a key to our life, home and ministry success.

To the women who read this book:
- These principles work. Operate them in diligence and submission to God's plan and He will confirm His word in your life.
- God is no respecter of persons (Acts 10:34). What he has done for us—he is obligated to do for you in principle. Be bold—Have faith that God will build a glorious home for you.

To the men who read this book:
- A godly woman is a precious gift with the divine potential inside her to build a glorious kingdom home; this book will help any women reach her full potential in the plan of God.
- God wants men who he can trust to protect, cultivate, and honor their wives as the princesses and divine daughters that they are. Your charge is to become a man that God can trust.
- The key principles in this book are for everyone—but you will see the maximum effect in your home & life if you are

pursuing Godliness with all your heart and encouraging your wife to do the same by example.

2 LIFE CHANGING PRAYERS

Prayer of Salvation

Father, I thank you for the precious gift of your son. In my heart, I believe that Jesus came to the earth, died and rose again for my sins. I ask you now Lord Jesus to come into my life, change my heart, and help me to live a life that pleases you. I receive you now as my Lord and my Savior. Thank you for coming into my heart and saving me, Lord Jesus. Amen.

Praise God! Make sure that you tell somebody that you have accepted Jesus into your heart and have made him your Lord and Savior. Next, as you look for a church to attend, ask the Lord to help you find one where His word is taught and modeled.

Prayer for Baptism of the Holy Spirit

Father, in Jesus name, I believe that when Your Son ascended into heaven that He sent the Holy Spirit to help me, lead me, guide me, teach me, and to empower me to do Your will. Holy Spirit, I yield myself to you. Come into my life, fill me, and baptize me with your power and anointing. I want the fullness of Your blessing. I receive your gifts into my life, right now. Thank You Father for your Son Jesus, and I now thank you for the gift of Your Holy Spirit and the evidence of that gift. Amen